VAAS
INQUISITI~~VENESS~~
& SOLUTIONS

DR. BHOJRAJ DWIVEDI

M.A. Phd. (Astrology)

DIAMOND BOOKS

ISBN : 81-7182-533-8

© Publisher

Publisher	:	**Diamond Pocket Books (Pvt.) Ltd.** X-30, Okhla Industrial Area, Phase - II, New Delhi-110020
Phone	:	011 - 51611861-865
Fax	:	011 - 51611866
E-mail	:	sales@diamondpublication.com
Website	:	www.diamondpublication.com
Edition	:	2004
Price	:	195/-
Price US$	:	14/-
Laser Typeset	:	Languagetron, Noida
Printed at	:	Adarsh Printers, Navin Shahdara, Delhi-32

Contents

Preface

Maximum number of books pertaining to, Vaastu Shastra, were written and published during the fag end of twentieth century and such books were printed in large quantity that it surpassed even the total number of books published in Astrology, Numerology, Palmistry, Omens and dreams. As popularity of Vedic Vaastu literature and Indian Vaastu science gained momentum, literature on 'Feng Shui' also did not lag behind, and became more prevalent and popular in the Western World. Foreign Scholars wrote so much on Feng Shui during the last five years that surpassed even the total number of books on the subject during the last century.

Present book is the 12th book on the Vaastu Science and if books on astrology, numerolagy, yantra-mantra-tantra etc. are also taken into account the aggregate comes to 128 books. A number of conferences, symposia, seminars, meetings and series of lectures were arranged to spread the cause, knowledge and awareness about Vaastu Shastra. Gooddess Saraswati is benevolent and kind to me, and it is due to her blessings that I have been able to write so many books on various subjects and also attend related conferences, pay Vaastu-visits in India and abroad, and my record still remains unsurpassed. I have been invited frequently to express my opinion on various facets of Vaastu and for this purpose I had to deliver audio-video interviews and lectures in India and abroad. I have been delivering lectures in various institutes like Lion's Club, Rotary Club, Inner Wheel, Saheli Club and other social and religious institutes in connection with personality development, orientation, time management, Astrology, Palmistry, significance and utility of Yagya (Sacrificed fire) and Vaastu. During the course of such conferences, interviews and interactions inquisitive people have been asking me many questions about the said subjects and I was supposed to convince them so that their desires and enquries are suitably addressed to. In addition, I also continue to receive letters, replete with various quarries, through mail and courier services, and also on phone and fax.

Some of the posers are highly interesting and enhance knowledge also. Shri Narendra Kumar Verma, Managing Director of Diamond Pocket Books (P) Ltd. has been insisting me to compile such questions and problems, relating to problems faced by the general public, so that such a compilation could be presented through a book. It is but natural that readers and inquisitive persons remain confronted with many inexplicable problems and all of them wish to

5

have suitable solution therefore. But there was a dearth of such books which could solve unsolved problems of general public. Hence, if a book is published on this subject it will dispel many unfounded and wrong conceptions, and serve as a guideline to the readers and general public. Hopefully, this book will fill in the gap in this direction and serve as a guideline.

I have closely read, studied and contemplated on a number of books on Vaastu Shastra, but none of the book has tackled ticklish subjects like 'Vedha' (Observation) and Door Planing, in which direction, I have made a constructive, practical and useful contribution. In fact, this is my pioneer effort which is unique and unsurpassed. I purchased so many books on Vaastu Shastra, but I was surprised and shocked to notice the authors have simply copied my diagrams and research oriented writings, as also pictures and gadgets. They have, in fact, represented my findings in their books and repeated the details given by me. Is it not immoral and improper to reprint my books under some other title? I filed cases of infringement of copyright. I also advised them that, if they have included my research based findings in their books, copied verbation also, they should, at least, express their courtesy and gratitude and also should not feel ashamed in conceding that they have reproduced my writings in their books. If they are sincerely honest, they could, at least, suitably compensate me in some other form. If they do so, it will help to maintain cordial relations and goodwill. But, it is regretted that such pseudo authors and cheap type of publishers refrains from doing so, because, if they do so, their personal ego will be adversely impacted, hence they preferred to take recourse to uncalled for clandestine and deceptive route. Amen!

'Vaastu Problems and solutions' is the first ever book on the subject wherein doubts of common man have been addressed to in the most suitable, practical, to the point way. The subject has been, so far, remained untouched and untapped and it is my bounden duty to dispel doubts and suggest practical and corrective ways to overcome this problem. First problem that confronts person is where to stock cement, stones, pebbles, iron and steel bars / material, wood etc. and nobody has touched upon this problem. There is also no guidance as to what should be the area of a plot of land, upon which a house is to be built, what should the proportion (Of covered and uncovered areas), and what results, whether good or bad, if a house is built in a particular direction. In addition, there is hardly or no mention about a stair case. So, such and many other problems are practical facts which I have tried to reply, so as to set at rest any misgivings and doubts. Similarly, the books are silent on the problem of 'boundary wall'.

There are countless and unlimited questions and problems and it is a herculean task to arrange them in order and classify them. Many readers also repeatedly seek clasifications on points which have already been replied. So, I have avoided repetitions, so as to make this book more poignant and purposeful. A book has a limited capacity to enable insertion of all the relevant points, as I have tried to explain the relevant facts by using miminal words. I have also given diagrams and pictures, where necessary, as they convey the importance which cannot be expressed, even by using a number of words. This is new approach and attempt which, I hope, our discerning readers will appreciate and take full advantage from the information provided therein. Further, each reader will find something new, according to his taste and necessity.

For the benefit of our enlightened readers, I am hereunder, giving my contact address so that the readers can contact our office, in case they have any Vaastu related problem. They can also write to me but it is not always physically possible to reply all the letters, even though our efforts and intention to reply to all the letters. There could be delay in replying, yet we try to reply to each and every letter. The readers are advised to attach a self-addressed and fully stamped envelope to our office and it is our moral duty to send a convincing reply to all their querries. Thanks and wishing a happy reading.

Dr. Bhojraj Dwivedi

Office :
International Vaastu Association (Regd.)
130, First 'A' Road, Marudeep Apartment,
Sardarpur, JODHPUR (Rajasthan, India)
Pin : 342 003
Phone : 0291-637359 (Office)
0291-431883 (Res.)

(I) Vaastu-Science in the Ambit of Questions

Q. What is meant by 'Vaastu'?

Ans. It is a word derived from Sanskrit language. It's root word is 'Vas' (वस्) and Tun (तुण) is a suffix—this is the linguistic etymology of 'Vaastu' which means—an art of house construction, built by a human being. It also protects a building from obstacles, natural calamities and upheavels.

In fact, Vaastu is the name of five elements, (like earth, water, space, air and wind) which remain united in a laiddown proportion & ratio, because proper balance amongst these five elements generate 'Bio-electric magnetic energy' which bestows excellent health, wealth, prosperity and comforts.

Q. How old (ancient) is Vaastu Science?

Ans. This question has been often inquired by many persons. Some critics says that Vaastu Science became popular and prevalent only a decade ago, which is not a factual conclusion. About 5000 years ago, Vaastu Science was in a advance stage during the Mahabharat era, as there is a detailed description of 'Town-Planning'. During the said era a demon, named Maya, was an adept person in architecture, who wrote a marvellous book, entitled 'Maya-Mahatamya' which is still available. Vishwakarma was a pioneer in Vaastu who consturcted Dwarka, a golden city, in the 'Dwapar' era. Sudama met Shri Krishan at the same place. According to lord Krishan's desire, golden city of Dwarka submerged into the sea. It is now famous as 'Bait Dwarka' (बेट द्वारका). He prophesied that in the 'Kaliyug' people will fight to possess gold, so he destroyed this golden city into fragments and himself submerged into the sea, so alongwith himself no trace of Lord Krishan and Dwarka city remains existent. About 21,65,095 years ago, lord Rama had used Vaastu Science at many places in the 'Treta' era (त्रेता युग). During this period the King of Lanka (Present Srilanka) installed the famous 'Jyotirlinga', at Rameshwar, as per Vaastu principles founded by Lord Rama. According to ancient testimony of the 'Puranas' Lord Shankar constructed a golden city, with his mental prowess, which was got installed by the scholar Ravan whom the lord donated it as a gift. But the golden Lanka got submerged into sea in due course of time. There are many references and commentaries about Vaastu Science and its principles.

9

There are also a number of mantras existing in the Vedas about 'Vaastu Shanti' (Pacification through Vaastu). Hence Vaastu is as ancient as the Vedas, so both the Vedas and Vaastu are everlasting.

Q. Which are the renowned ancient treatises and books on ancient Vaastu Science?

Ans. According to 'Matsaya Puran' names of 18 scholars are mentioned who discoursed on Vaastu Science.

भृगुरत्रि वसिष्ठश्च विश्वकर्मा मयस्तथा॥

नारदो नग्न जित्वैव विशालक्ष: पुरन्दर:॥

ब्रह्म कुमारो नन्दीश: शौनको गर्ग एव च।

वास्तु देवोऽनिरुद्धश्च तथा शुक्र बृहस्पति॥

[Bhriguratri Vashishthashcha Vishwakarma Mayastatha Naardo Nagan Jivaaiva Vishalaksha Purandarah,

Brahma Kumaro Nandeeshah Shaunako Garg Eva cha,

Vaastu devo Aniuddhoshacha Tatha Shukra Brihaspati.]

1. Bhrigu 2. Attri 3. Vashistha 4. Vishwakarma 5. Maya 6. Narad 7. Naganjit 8. Vishalakhsha 9. Purandar 10. Brahma 11. Kumar 12. Nandish 13. Shaunak 14. Garg 15. Vasudev 16. Aniruddha 17. Shukra and 18. Brihaspati are the names of eighteen pioneer scholars of Vaastu Shastra.

Q. Is it a necessity to study Vaastu Shastra?

Ans. Origin of Vaastu Shastra is motivated by the spirit of welfare of humanity and justification of life. The scholar Vishwakarma, a renowned architect of ancient times expresses himself as follows:

"वास्तुशास्त्र प्रविक्ष्यामि लोकानां हित काम्यया।

आरोग्य पुत्रलाभं धनं धान्यं लभ्येन्नरा॥

[Vaastu Shastra Pravikshyami Lokanam Hit Kamyaya,

Arogya Putralabham Cha Dhanam Dhanyam Labhennarah]

That is to say that a person gains excellent health, freedom from diseases, birth of sons, wealth, property and high class luxuries, by studying the science of Vaastu. People all over the world deem the construction of buildings as a worldly act, while in India it is deemed as an act of religiosity. An architect can, no doubt, construct an excellent building but cannot guarantee a comfortable life to the dwellers, who reside in such buildings, whereas knowledge of Vaastu Science assures a guarantee in this respect.

Q. Has Indian art of Vaastu remained neglected?

Ans. Though Indian Vaastu art is highly popular in the western world but, it is also a fact that it remained neglected in its own country of origin. In the ancient times all the palatial and big royal palaces, forts, temples, educational

10

institutes, ponds, wells, water tanks and gardens/orchards and dwelling houses were constructed in accordance with the directions given in Vaastu and architectural sciences. But gradually rising population, paucity of land and pieces of plots, flat system and western impact and blind copy of this civilisation's haywere and dazzling appearance caused immense damage to Indian Vaastu and architecture, hence its decline and resultant deformity in its place of origin.

Q. How ancient is Vedic Vaastu Science?

Ans. Some critics says that Vaastu Shastra is only a decade old, but this is a baseless acusation. Even 5000 years ago Vaastu science existed in its most developed form in the Mahabharat era, where detailed description of this science with regard to building construction is available. During this very period Maya, a renowned and adept Vaastu expert existed, who wrote an outstanding book, entitled 'Maya-Mahatamya' which is available even now. I have already given a detailed account in the preceding pages as to how Dwarka, Lanka, Rameshwar, etc. were built in complete conformity with Vaastu principles and directions. Hence Vaastu is as ancient as old as our Vedas are.

I. Some Facts & Features of Vaastu

Q. Is Vaastu Science meant to serve the purpose of the rich and elite class? Do not such Vaastu guidelines apply in the case of a poorman's hut?

Ans. I often receive letters where it has been alleged that Vaastu benefit accrue only to industrialists, factories, shops, large residential and high-rise buildings, but its benefits do not percolate to poor and lower strata of society. This is a baseless accusation with regard to Vaastu Science. For instance sunlight and sun-rays, cold or hot winds do not distinguish between the rich and the poor, because all of them are equally impacted by light, Sun and wind and the amount of benefits derived is also the same. Similarly balance or imbalance between five elements (earth, water, fire, space and wind) also affects all the classes of society alike and without any discrimination, hence Vaastu science is also meant for equal benefit of all the human beings. But, it depends on the efficiency and capability of a person, whether he is rich or poor, to derive benefit from this unique science.

I would like to refer to an interesting and reliable testimony (proofs in respect of construction of a cottage/hut from Ramayana.) Lord Rama was exiled and Lakshman built a grass or thatched cottage for Rama, where there was suitable provision for free entry of light and air; as per the Vasstu guidelines. When lord Rama saw the cottage he was thrilled to see a Vaastu-based cottage.

He remarked -

'कर्तव्यं वास्तुशमनं सौमित्र चिरंजीवी भव'।

(श्री वाल्मीकि रामायणे। अयोध्या काण्डे। 56/श्लोक 22

[Kartavyam Vaastu Shamnan Saummitrey Chiranjeev Bhava.

(Quoted from Shri Valmiki Ramayana/Ayodha Kaand/56/Verse 22)

Which means, "O Lakshman! We will worship and perform a sacrifice to honour the founder of Vaastu, (Vaastu deity) in this thatched hut". Because the persons who desire a longer span of life, must resort to Vaastu pacification (Vaastu Shanti). Is there any proof required about the utility and authenticity of Vaastu science?

Q. Should Vaastu factor be taken into account even in the case of rented house?

Ans.: I receive a number of such letters in which the readers often ask such questions. People generally ask what is the utility and justification of Vaastu and its applicability as they are living in rented houses, and also that they will remain free from damaging impact of defective Vaastu. I advise such inquisitive readers that if there is a hole in a boat, whether its owned or rented by the travellers, it will equally harm all the boarders, whether they are owners or not. In the similar matter, if Vaastu of a house is faulty, it will cast its ill impact on all the inmates who dwell in such a house and it hardly matters whether they are tenants or owners in the house, as calamaties do not distinguish between an owner and a tenant. So, great attention should be paid to Vaastu rules in residential houses, whether the occupant is an owner or a tenant.

Q. Some industries, factories or houses remain partly constructed and never completed. Why is it so?

Ans. This problem we often witness in our practical life that construction work on some factories is started but left incomplete midway. There can also be seen some houses where first floor was completed but further construction had to be stopped. There are also certain houses whose structure was built, but could not be plastered. If plaster work is complete, painting is incomplete. There are also houses where doors, windows and decoration still needed to be completed. In some cases no money was left to complete the house or shop, and paucity of funds was the only snag. After all why such problems emerge? Such problems surface due to non-performance of land purification. The plot owner did not perform rituals with regard to land purification, worship, digging and construction work was not started on an auspicious day and time. Such problems would not have occurred nor any difficulty arisen if the house owner

12

had followed the above mentioned preconditions of Vaastu. Hence, before initiating any type of construction, it is very imperative that Vaastu requirments are fully complied with.

Q. Does Vaastu Shastra apply and affect the Hindus only or has it any impact on Christians or Muslims?

Ans. I wrote a series of articles under the caption 'Sarita Ki Vaastu Virodhi Dhara Pravaha' whereunder such questions were raised and replied to. Effect of sunlight is cast upon the Hindus, Muslims and Christians alike and without any discrimination. But all the persons are not endowed with identical wisdom and understanding. I will quote here the story of five blind persons and an elephant. When they touched the elephant, a person caught hold of elephant's tail, the second one his trunk, the third one placed his hand on the ear, the foruth person held the animal's back and other one caught its foot firmly. One who caught the tail, felt that the elephant is like a broom, one who caught the trunk declared that the elephant is like an inverted fountain, because it is thick on the upper side but thin on the lower side, the person who touched the ear, said it resembles like a fan, one who caught the foot said it looks like a pole and the last one said it is like a mountain. Each person's conclusion was based only on one portion of the animal, hence there is a seeming incongruity which denotes a limited and restricted vision which is confined only to one aspect, hence the variations give inconclusive descriptions.

In order to seek protection from scorching heat of the sun, one took shelter under roof of a temple, the second one went to nearest mosque, the third one took rest under a Gurudwara, the fourth one rested under a Pyramid and the fifth one took protection under an umbrella. Motive of all the said persons was identical, but only the sources were different.

All the castes, religions and communities are divided throughout the world, hence each one of them has its individual parameters with regard to architecture and art of Vaastu, and the variations depict different outlook of each civilization. Every Civilization has its own measuring rods and beliefs. Despite all this, there is no Civilization in the world which does not believe in architecture, Vaastu art and knowledge about house/building construction. Prof. Talbore Hemlin, Professor in the department of architecture, at American university, wrote a 700 Page voluminous book which was published at New York in 1838, wherein he has given detailed account of Culture of Egyptians, Roman, East-West Asia, Unani, Japanese, Muslim and Christian architecture and Vaastu science. He has also described relevant rules of each of the cultures and sciences of architecture and Vaastu, and has also given pictures in support of his assertions. Hence it is a figment of falsehood to declare that Vaastu knowledge exists only in India and the Hindus, rather each civilization has its own literature in this regard.

Hindus believe that eastern direction is venerable, carries much weight as glimpse of the rising sun can be had in the eastern direction only. Moreover, early glimpse of the rising Sun in the morning imparts new direction of life, energy, and it also motivates them to start work on a happy note. As the Sun is the leading deity of the Hindus, they have built their temples that face the eastern side. The Muslims worship the setting sun, hence western direction is venerable for them, as the sun sets in the west. They believe that rays of the setting sun are more cooler, and cool rays mollify scorching heat and also tone down thirst, and thus provide much respite to the Aalis So, the Muslims keep their mosques facing the west, because Kaba also faces this direction. All muslim brethren strictly follow the concept of western direction and its piety, though modern medical science and ultra science also subscribe to and support the Hindu view-point.

Ancient Egyptian Culture has proved that anything kept under a Pyramid will remain as it is, since it never gets distorted. The same system applies to tombs of Hindu temples, rather the principles of phonology are more resonant in tombs of temples, since the idol, installed under a tomb, always remains awakened. Experiencing and sensing the peculiar features of Hindu tombs, the Muslims adopted this pattern and demonstrated it by making holes in the tomb— they copied in totality but they eyed merely on the beauty of tombs, but could not understand the underlying purpose for which the tombs were built. I shall be discussing about ancient Egyptian Vaastu Science and modern Pyramidal therapeutic approach in the next chapter.

Q. Can Vaastu faults be rectified without breakage?

Ans. Many inquisitive readers often ask that if kitchen, toilet, bathroom are built in faulty method in a house, factory, shop or industry, can such faults be dispelled without breaking them? In this respect, my opinion is that those Vaastu experts, who advise too much of breakage at a factory site, are actually **naives and novices**. I have myself seen that in big metro cities, like Delhi, Mumbai, Kolkata, Chennai etc. many families live only in a single room which consists of bedroom, worshiproom, bathroom, toilet, Kitchen etc. In such a situation a person's, family has to live in a single room, flat due lack of facility and resources for building an independent house, there is hardly any scope for breakage. But, even then, it is advisable to correct the fault pertaining to fire, water, worship place, safe vault, and sleeping room. Even after doing this

14

much, there will still be left many other faults in a building which should be rectified, but it is generally not possible due to some practical factors. In order to remove other residuary Vaastu faults, we have processed 16 types of Ganesh Emulets which are nomeclated as 'Vaastu Dosha Shayan Yantra', 'Sarvamangal Vaastu Yantra', 'Varun Yantra', 'Shri Yantra', 'Kali Yantra', 'Bagula Yantra', 'Maruti Yantra', 'Siddha Beesa Yantra', 'Indrani Yantra', etc. which are highly effective and efficacious. Our clients have used these yantras, according to Vaastu defects, and have reaped benefits. Hence, breakage is not necessary, what actually required is the advice and guidance of an experienced Vaastu expert. But do not be misled by pseudo and self proclaimed so called Vaastu scholars, who have immense capacity to harm and damage the interests of innocent aspirants.

On 14/15-12-1996 we founded the foundation of International Vaastu Sammelan and held a congregation to impart knowledge, guidance to the general public and also with a view to assemble the learned scholars on Vaastu on one stage. Under the aegies of Lions' club of Delhi, a gathering of scholarly Vaastu experts was arranged at Hotel Taj, Delhi, and it was a grand Success.

Q. Our house has been built in violation of the Vaastu rules, even then we are happy and prosperous! What is the reason?

Ans. Such claims are analogous to the fact that some people are atheists and do not obey their parents, even then they are happy and prosperous. Such persons are actually deceiving and misleading others. For instance a person is having cancer but he is unaware of his malady and he is happy till his disease is not detected. Once correct diagnosis has been made and results disclosed to him, he will sail in troubled waters. So, a person having adverse vaastu, is happy and prosperous, until his stars are favourable and lucky and his good stars favour him.

As soon as planetary position changes and situation turns hostile, he will get embroiled in a mess of problematic difficulties and shall not be able to extricate himself out of the advertsities. Resultantly his life will become miserable. Two things affect a person, Vaastu (50%) and luck (50%). If stars are benefic and Vaastu is defective, then the yield will only be 50% as compared to efforts put in (that is he will put in double effort than is required in a normal courses). But, conversely if Vaastu is blemishless but stars are unfavourable, results will not be that adverse, as compared to the situation when both Vaastu and stars are adverse. It implies that, if a house is constructed according to Vaastu principles, then the favourable planetary position can also change for the better.

15

Q. How many books have you written on Vaastu Science and other subjects and how many have been published, so far?

Ans. In all I have written 128 books on Karma Kand and Vaastu and all have been published, in addition to books in English translation. It is heartening to note that the discerning readers have approbated all my books. I continue to receive letters from my readers who all encourage me to write more books on such subjects.

Q. What are your plans for the future?

Ans. I plan to record and release Audio-Video Cassettes of my series of lectures.

Q. Do you personally pay Vaastu-visits at sites?

Ans. Yes, I continue to receive invitations for visiting hotels, factories, multi-storayed buildings, industries, commercial complexes and houses. I try my best to meet the demands of my inquisitive and appreciative readers and try to solve their problems but, at times, I cannot pay a Vaastu-visit due to time crunch.

Q. How is it that satisfactory efforts are still found wanting in respect of propagation and popularity of Vaastu related education and knowledge?

Ans. Indian Vaastu science is far more popular in the foreign countries, as Indian astrology and Vaastu Science are taught in foreign universities, but the Indian government is apathetically indifferent in this regard.

Q. What is the utility and justification for arranging conferences to spread the knowledge of Vaastu Science?

Ans. Vaastu conferences, training camps, presentation of research papers and publication therof, no doubt, help a lot in furthering the cause of spread of Vaastu knowledge and they also serve the desired purpose. In addition, such meetings also add to knowledge of the participants.

Q. How many conferences have been held so far?

Ans. First Vaastu Conference was held at Bangalore in the legislative assembly, on 4 & 5 June, 1995 and Dr. B.V. Raman was invited. The Conference was presided over by Shri Deva Gowda, the then Prime Minister, Chief Election Commissioner Shri T.N. Sheshan and the former Chief Minister, Shri Ram Krishna Hegde. I also presented and read a paper as a special invitee and was also awarded, 'Vishwakarma Award'. The second conference was held between January 23 and 25, 1996 at Baroda University in Gujarat state, and I chaired and presided over the conference one day, and Shri Nalin Bhatt, the education minister of Gujarat government was the chief guest. Both the said conferences

16

were at the national level, but the next one will be at international level.

Q. How many conferences have been arranged, so far, by your institute?

Ans. Our institute has been working in respect of Astrological and other such sciences for the past 15 years. Under the aegies of our institute following conferences have, so far been held which are credited with historical achievements.

1982 (Jodhpur), 1983 (Modinagar), 1984 (Delhi), 1986 (Jodhpur), 1987 (Saharanpur), 1992 (Jodhpur), 14-15 December, 1996 (Jodhpur), 1997 (Mumbai), 1998 (Hardwar), 1998 (Udaipur), 1998 (Ahmedabad), 1998 (Jodhpur), 1998 (Kathmandu, Nepal), 20-12-1998 (Jodhpur), 8 to 9 January 2000 (Juhu, Mumbai), October 2000 (Egypt).

Q. When the next conference will be held?

Ans. Next international Vaastu Sammelan will held on 24 & 25 January, 2001 at Ravindra Manch, Bhopal (M.P). It will consist of eight sessions and all the relevant Vaastu related subjects will be broadly discussed at each session.

Q. Is your institute arranging for a conference in a Foreign Country?

Ans. Yes, the next Vaastu Conferenct will take place at Nairobi, the capital of Kenya.

Q. Why Vaastu Science is so popular these days?

Ans. India's Ram and Krishn were exported to foreign countries and they made their comeback in the form of 'Rama' and 'Krishna' and Patanjali's Yog eturned to India in the form of 'Yoga', and these changed names were greeted and received with open arms in India on their Comeback trail. The same story applies to Indian Vaastu Science also, which is also highly popular in foreign countries like 'Rama', 'Krishna' and 'Yoga'.

Foreigners were fed up with unplanned houses and high rise buildings and they were feeling tormented and restive in such concrete structures. So, they turned to Indian Vaastu Shastra and adopted it, resultantly they praised this unique science and its popularity and significance was carried forward by books in foreign languages and media — it also cast a salutary impact on Indian inteligentia and scholarly writers awakened and religion proned writers started writing books due to which 'Matsya Purana', 'Agni Purana', 'Mayanitan', 'Samvagan Sutra' were translated in English and other foreign languages. During the last five years so much literature has flooded the market in respect of Vaastu literature) that people found it difficult to choose the most suitable book—mushroom growth of Vaastu literature not only started and awakened the Indian readers but it sent favourable signals to the western

17

world. Due to all the said factors, Vaastu has gained more popularity than astrology even.

Q. How can a person acquire more information about Vaastu Shastra?

Ans. These days many people desire to know about more factual and substantive information about Vaastu and such a demand is progressively rising. Due to flood of books on the subject, people are in a fix about the choice of the most suitable book which could satiate their curiosity. I have been asked a number of times whether there is some course on the subject. In order to meet ever growing demand of our clients we have started two distant education courses each of six month's duration which are conducted through correspondance. Any desirous person can take up these courses. We also confer honorary degrees / diplomas of 'Vaastu Vidya Visharad' and 'Vaastu Markand', apart from imparting relevant & requisite knowledge on the subject.

Q. How more information can be had about Feng Shui?

Ans. You can read our book enlitled 'Feng Shui' Chinese Vaastu Shastra is available in Hindi and English (Published by Diamond Pocket Books) and you will yourself realize, after reading the book, as to how easy it is to learn and know Feng Shui.

Q. Can a person practise in Vaastu or Feng Shui after reading relevant books?

Ans. Of course, you can. But it would be still better to complete our prescribed course and then take to practice. But, you must also have a Vaastu teacher whose blessings and guidance should be sought, as his timely guidance will pave the way for your quicker success.

Q. Being ancient Sciences, can Vaastu and Feng Shui take care of and prove useful in the existing (modern) life-style?

Ans. Howsoever ancient any science may be, it cannot be oblivious to new changes, conditions, life-style etc. Model of thinking and utility may change, but the basic concepts remain unchanged. For instance, ancient conjuctions of Indian astrology Viz. 'Ashwa Yoga' and 'Gajayoga' have been replaced by modern cars and vehicles. Old hearth has been replaced by L.P.G. stove, but the element of fire remains even now unchanged. Similarly old Bhatti (Kiln) has been replaced by a furnaces / electric heater or boilor, but utility of each item remains unchanged. But it is also a fact that gas stove hearth or Kiln should always be in the south-east direction (Agni-Kon) Hence Vaastu science is more relevant now in the context of modern life style.

Q. Is Feng Shui meant for the Chinese Only?

Ans. Indian Vaastu Science is incompatible. No science can match it. If Vaastu and Feng Shui are studied side-by-side, you will yourself come to know the difference, because truth requires no proof.

Q. Do Vaastu and / or Feng Shui believe in and motivated by magic or blind faith?

Ans. Not at all.

Q. After Vaastu fault removal, how long does it take to feel and experience effect of results.

Ans. It takes three days, fortyfive days or three months to experience the benefits of changes, after complying with Vaastu rules and rituals.

Q. Is the utility of Vaastu confined only to the Concept of a comfortable dwelling house?

Ans. A comfortable house or building is only one of the many advantages of Vaastu but it also consists of a comfortable and prosperous family life of all the inmates, their happiness and all round welfare.

Q. Does Vaastu science affect the life of all the inmates in a family?

Ans. Certainly, it casts its affects on the head of the family and the rest of members in a family. If the house owner is happy and prosperous, all other family members will also be happy and prosperous but, if he himself is under trouble and tormented, other family members will also have similar impact.

Q. If I introduce minor changes, then what would the effect?

Ans. Yes, it will also cast its impact in a limited capacity only, because benefits derived will be in proportion to the changes introduced. But, if a house is fully free from Vaastu faults, it will show hundred percent good effects. Hence, it implies that even minor changes will also show results, but to a limited extent only.

Q. Does it cost a lot to invite a Vaastu expert for a Vaastu visit?

Ans. It is only a fallacy, as it costs a merely 1/2 per cent cost of total construction of a house, which is quite a negligible expenses, as compared to the advantages. Even then, it all depends on the Vaastu expert's experience and efficiency and it varies from man to man; as payment made to an experienced and capable Vaastu expert could be higher than the payment made to a pseudo and novice person. Hence, the house owners should thrash out all the relevant modalities, lest there emerges any misunderstanding later on.

Q. Is it possible to seek Vaastu remedies by way of correspondance also?

Ans. Yes, most of the Vaastu faults can be corrected and remedied through correspondence also. But the house owner must send his house-plan (map), and northern direction should be succinctly denoted by an arrow mark. If house-plan is actual, there is no need for a Vaastu-visit.

Q. What's the difference between correspondence and a Vaastu-visit?

Ans. Sometimes, map of a house varies with actual construction of a house or some changes might have been taken place after drawing of final house plan. Further, northern direction is wrongly marked in the house plan. Such anomalies can only be detected at the time of Vaastu-visit, as in 60% cases northern direction is marked erroneously. But, when a personal visit is made, all such and other anomalies come to the fore and detected. Even the environs cannot be ascertained without a personal visit and interior decoration can also be noticed when a personal visit is paid. Hence Vaastu-visit has many advantages.

Q. Is there any guarantee that the suggested remedial steps will yield desired benefits?

Ans. When we visit any doctor, we do not seek any guarantee as to whether the patient would be fully cured or he will not die. But when we visit a doctor, we have the confidence that the doctor will cure the malady. Hence faith and confidence are the two essential ingredients to attain any relief. Remember, lack of confidence can never generate faith. Hence, it is pre requisite to have an unswerving faith in the treatises and the scholarly Vaastu expert.

Q. Can I become lucky by dint of a Vaastu experts advice and guidance?

Ans. Of course, But able and experienced Vaastu experts are rarely to be found. If such people are available luck can certainly take a turn for the better by their advice. It is a source of good luck that a scholarly, experienced and expert Vaastu scholar visits your house, because his entry in the house will improve your fortune.

Q. Is it imperative to cause breakage in the house, according to Vaastu expert's counsel?

Ans. It is not at all, essential because only the novices will advise for such an (uncalled for) action. My book, entitled 'Remedial Vaastu Shastra' is sufficient testimony to the fact that changes could be affected even without causing breakage to the existing building and many people have benefitted from our advice given in the said book and we continue to receive letter from our readers but only in 5% of the cases, we cannot compromise, because of the faulty eastern and north-eastern direction.

Q. To what extent Vaastu advice can affect my present life-style?

Ans. Vaastu related advice can bring an overhauling change in your life-style. It will bestow spiritual energy, motivate you towards God worship, by giving you positive thinking. But, it all depends on your own capability as to how and what extent you can translate Vaastu expert's advice in your practical life. So, the success rate will conform to the quantan of your compliance and adherance to his advice.

Q. Is Vaastu advice essential for interior decoration?

Ans. Yes, it is absolutely essential. Interior decoration, if faulty, will spoil the entire spectrum, if a house is designed and built in accordance with Vaastu rules—it is like a handsome and healthy person wearing dirty and discoloured clothes. I know a person could not enjoy a sound sleep in his bedroom, due to faulty interior decoration.

Q. Can change of furniture in a house also change a person's fortune?

Ans. Yes, furniture is an essential and integral part of interior decoration and this aspect has been accorded a thoughtful and serious consideration in ancient (Vedic) Indian Vaastu Science. What kind of wood should be used for beds, in which direction chairs, sofa set should be placed, where to keep the study table, what colour will suit boundary-wall, walls and curtains, what should be an ideal shape of a dining table and what are the appropriate places where dining table, T.V., telephone, heater, cooler, refrigerators, washing machine etc. should be kept, what should be the design and shape of furniture—these facts have been suitably dealt within Vaastu Science.

A gentleman always thought correctly while he was in the office but, as soon as he returned to his home, he used to change his decisions. He remained easy, happy and relaxed in his office, but as soon as he returned to his house, there was strife, discomfort and trouble. During my Vaastu—visit to his house, I advised him to change his furniture. He did as advised and complete happiness returned to him, as change of the furniture changed his entire thinking also. When colour of walls and curtains is changed, it will affect improvement in stars and fortune, because colours cast great impact on the colours emanated by the stars.

Q. Can wrong Vaastu advice cause adverse impact?

Ans. Certainly, a wrong advice will cast ill impact, as a wrong medicine, given by a doctor, will worsen a patient's condition. Hence, it is a stupendous task and factual problem to find out a really able and conscientious Vaastu expert out of the crowd of novice Vaastu experts.

Q. Can the devices (Yantra) suggested to remove Feng Shui and Vaastu faults, cause adverse impact?

21

Ans. No, certainly not, because all these emulets do not cast any adverse impact / reaction. The situation can be compared to allopathic medicines which, if prescribed wrongly, will certainly cause reaction, but homeopathic medicines never (or rarely) react. For instance, if sugar is added to milk or water, it will sweeten both the liquids. Similarly all the Yantras, suggested to dispel any Vaastu defect and fault, will always impart positive results, because they are replete with positive energy, hence there can never be any adverse effect, because negative energy never flows through them.

Q. Can you cite any example of any building which has been built in complete accordance with Feng Shui or Vaastu rules?

Ans. So many buildings exist in India and foreign countries which are built strictly according to Vaastu / Feng Shui directions and rules. But, it is not possible to give exact number of such buildings as it is like asking a person to count and name the buildings over which sun rays fall. Even then I can refer to 'Pushya Nakshatra Bhawan' at Jodhpur, 'Mehran Garh' fort of Jodhpur, Ummed Bhawan, are brilliant examples of Indian Vaastu Science architecture.

Q. Is Feng-Shui science confined only to design and interior decoration of a building?

Ans. House, shop, mansion, temple, factory, hotels etc. have been dealt with in considerable details in Feng Shui, in addition to dealing with changes in interior decoration. There are also discussions on improving a person's fortune, his prosperity and comforts. So, it is a multi-faceted science, hence it cannot be labelled a science that deals with interior decoration only; as its object and canvas are quite wide.

Q. Has interior decoration and colours any relation to the stars and zodiac signs?

Ans. Interior decoration and colours have direct relationship with stars and their impact on the stars, and it has been confirmed and we have referred to these affects many a time. Colour of the Sun is golden yellow and orange, that of the Moon is pearl / white, Colour of Mars is coral-red, Mercury is green, Jupiter is yellow, Venus is bright white, Saturn is black or deep blue, dragon's head is brown / grey and that of dragon's tail is mixed with stripes. Colour of the personal room and internal room of the house-owner, will denote by which star he is affected and what is ascendant and Zodiac sign.

Q. Does the science of Feng Shui also accord any importance to stars, in relation to interior decoration and colours?

Ans. Like the Indian Vaastu science, Feng Shui also attaches importance to interior decoration and role of stars, but in a limited extent only. There are also fixed colours to be used separately for each room in Feng Shui.

Q. Does Feng Shui also subscribe to the role of stars in determining the colours and interior decoration?

Ans. This is corollary of the preceding question which has already been explained. The house-owner should use the same colour in his drawing room which corresponds to colour attributed to the lord of his zodiac sign or the colour of the most dominant and favourable star (as ascertained from the birth horoscope) should be used in the bedroom and drawing room, so that he can gain from vibrations generated by the positive rays. He should not use any curtain, picture or cover of an inimical star's colour in his bedroom or drawing-room, as it is bound to adversely impact his decisions and happiness. If a person, born in cancer ascendant, should use deep blue, black or indigo colour in his drawing-room, it will constitute 'Vishayoga'. If the colour of walls is brown/grey or catechu or spotted/speckled, it will constitute 'Grahan Yoga', as a result of which he will always remain worried—these are the clear indications and beliefs of Indian Vaastu science.

Q. Is Dragon a Symbolic expression / sign of Feng-Shui?

Ans. Undoubtedly, Dragon is the symbolic and representative symbol of Feng Shui, in the same way as Ganpati is the representative symbol of Vedic Vaastu.

Q. Name the other representative symbols in Indian Vaastu science and Feng Shui.

Ans. In addition Ganpati, Swastik, Bell, Onkar, Lotus, Conch, Bowers, Vessel, Coconut, Panch Pallava's wall paintings are considered as auspicious symbols in Vedic Vaastu. Similarly, Pakua Mirror, Kailloon, Three Cows, Red Ribbon, White Tiger, Tortoise, Phoenix, Love Bird, Yin, Yang are some of the prominent symbols in Feng Shui and these are now popular everywhere.

Q. How many 'Animal Signs' are existent according to chinese astrology?

Ans. According to the chinese astrology there are twelve Zodiac signs, like 1) Mouse 2) Bull / Ox 3) Lion 4) Hare 5) Dragon 6) Snake 7) Horse 8) Goat 9) Monkey 10) Cock 11) Dog and 12) Pig.

Q. How it can be determined that a person is born in which animal zodiac sign?

Ans. Animal signs can be determined through the Chinese lunar calendar year. That is a person is born in which sign can only be ascertained through the said calendar.

Q. To what extent is the Chinese animal sign authentic?

23

Ans. Chinese 12 Zodiac (animal) signs are copied from Indian astrology's 12 Zodiac Signs; and a person's nature will correspond to that of the animal (sign) under which he was born. For further details you may refer to my book, entitled 'Feng Shui' — Chinese Vaastu Shastra, (Published by Diamond Pocket Books), and you will gain all the relevant information about Chinese Feng Shui science.

Q. Are Indian Zodiac Signs more rebiable and authentic or Chinese animal signs?

Ans. In their own each system is precise and correct. Indian Zodiac sings can be seen directly in the sky; hence Indian system is more scientific.

Q. What is the importance of directions in Vaastu Science.

Ans. Construction of a building is made on the basis of directions so that the land / house owner may derive following benefits—

1. It may prove auspicious and profitable.
2. Bless the owner with progeny (male).
3. Wealth, property, comforts, happiness and enjoyment may increase.

(II) Types of Land and Land Examination

Q. What are reasons and justifications for earmarking directions in respect of building construction?

Ans. Construction of a building should be in such a way that it should ensure following benefits, viz **Advantage of Sunrays** — House should be built in such a way that Sun-rays should enter a house uninterrupted and the house-owner should be able to enjoy the advantages of Sun-rays, even while he is sitting within his house. This is the reason as to why eastern direction has been accorded such a significant position in house construction.

Advantage of Mangnetic rays. Earth is like a magnet, and magnetic rays emanate from the north pole and human body gets affected by these rays. Every constructed building on earth is like a small magnet. So, a building should he constructed in such a way that magnetic rays could enter a house without any obstacles and also that the house-owner is able to derive benefits of such rays even while he is sitting within his house—this is the reason as to why the northern part of a house is kept low.

Since North and eastern directions should be kept at low plinth, hence north-eastern part is kept at low plinth. Similarly, great importance is attached to water, fire, worship-room, bed-room, gates, main / royal gate etc. and all are arranged for in designated directions only. In addition to the aforesaid factors, air and sunlight should enter through which direction, free entry of unhindered air, light, how water and fire should be provided and arranged, how the house-owner should enjoy a sound and comfortable sleep are the other factors which are accorded top priority so that the inmates of the house are able to enjoy a healthy, prosperous and comfortable life and also that they are blessed with a disease-free health, status, male progeny, wealth, and other requirements of life.

Q. What are the types of land?

Ans. It has been mentioned in this connection—

सुगन्धा ब्राह्मणी भूमि, रक्तगन्धा तु क्षत्रिया।
मधुगन्धा भवेद्वैशैया मद्यगन्धा चशूद्रिका॥

[Sugandha Brahmani Bhoomi, Raktaganda Tu Khshatriya,
Madhgandha Bhavedavaishya, Madyagandha ch Shoodrika.

Meaning : The land that smells like fragrance is a Brahman land, that which smells like the blood is a Khshatriya land, which smells like the honey is

25

a Vaishya land and the one that smells like urine is a Shudra land.

Q. What are the characteristic features of each type of land detailed heretofore?

Ans. Characteristics of each type of land (Earth) are briefly described hereunder.

1) Brahman Land

This type of land is replete with fragrant smell, has white dust (earth), contains sweet water and Kusha grass (sacred grass) grows over it.

2) Khahatriya Land

It's soil smell like blood and its colour is red, its water is astringent, 'Munja, type of grass grows over it'.

3) Vaishya Land

This type of land smells like rice grains, its soil is green, its water is citree and 'Kush' grass grows over its soil.

4) Shudra Land

This type of land's soil smells like wine, its soil is black, its water is bitter and all types of grass grow over here.

Land examination is carried out on the basis of the above mentioned types of land / soil.

Q. What are the other criteria / measuring rods for inspection and examination of land?

1) Land-examining by digging a pit

The land-owner should dig a one yard deep and one yard brood and then follow the following method to examine the land, after the land lord has filled in the pit with the same dust.

			Result
i)	a)	If amount of dust is less	It is ominous
	b)	If it neither increases nor decreases	It is normal
	c)	If it increases	It is auspicious
ii)	Fill water in the pit and the house-owner should walk upto 100 steps and then return to the same place.		
	a)	If water content neither increases nor decreases	It is auspicious
	b)	If water content decreases	It is ominous
iii)	Dig a pit at the time of sunset and fill it with water, then again visit the site in the morning.		

26

and if—
 a) If residual water remains   It is auspicious
 b) If there is no residual water   It is normal
 c) If land cracks   It is ominous

2) If you wish to perform some rituals and wish to erect a canopy and 'Yagya Kunda' (a spot in an iron pot in which sacrificial fire is ignited), the land-owner should be accompanied by five Brahmin priests and all should proceed to the site on an auspicious day and time. If there is any blade of grass, uproot the same. Then dig a knee-deep pit and fully fill the same with water and chant mantras to seek good actions and benevolence. Next morning visit the site again, see the pit and watch if—

a) The soil cracks or there are bones, it is not a suitable land for dwelling, as it will lessen the age of the owner and also destroy his wealth.
b) The land develops pits, the land is thorny and there is termite also, then this type of land ought to be abandoned at the first instance.
c) Some quantity of residual water is seen, it is an auspicious land.
d) There is no water left, it is a mediocre type of land.

Examination of land during digging operation and effect of the dug out articles.

If a piece of land is dug up for the purpose of land examination and following types of articles are dug up, then one should be guided by the following results.

Articles dug up	Result / effect
1. Termite, snake, Pipal etc.	Not fit for living, inauspicious
2. Sea-Shells, Rope	Distress, Strife
3. Egg, Serpent, Chaff, Husk	Death-like tormentation
4. Cut pieces of Cloth	Grave Misery
5. Burnt Charcoal / Coal	Cause of disease
6. Beggar's bowl	Feuds and Strife
7. Iron products	Death of the landlord
8. Bones, Skull, Hair etc.	End to the life of the landlord.
9. Conch, Shell, Tortoise etc.	Prosperity, mirth
10. Stones	Benefit of gold
11. Brick	Prosperity
12. Coins	Excellent comforts and prosperity
13. Copper	Increase in prosperity and affluence

Q. What factors should be taken into account before a piece of land is purchased?

Ans. The prospective buyer of land should minutely study the following factors, before he decides to purchase land as **Subtle and thorough examination of piece of land.**

Before a buyer decides to purchase a piece of land, he must closely and thoroughly survey the environment, atmosphere and general conditions prevailing on an around the prospective site. He should make sure that following points are fully examined.

Air — He should stand at the site, breathe in the open atmosphere and note whether he feels worse or better.

Plants —Examine thoroughly the plants growing on the soil.

Animals — What kind of animals roam on the land and how they act, move and behave—take this factor in active consideration before you decide to purchase any piece of land.

If the environs are pleasing and favourable, your mind is happier, you feel better, then only purchase that piece of land, otherwise not. It will still be better, if an experienced Vaastu expert is engaged for the purpose and his advice followed.

Q. Which type of site is liable to be discarded according to Vaastu?

Ans. According to Vaastu conical sites are not deemed good and auspicious and should not be purchased for building construction. A plot, which is traingular, round, north-east direction is cut or nutilated, south-east direction is extended, south-east corner is extended towards south, western side is extended towards south-west direction, west is extended in the direction of north-west corner and north portion is also extended towards north-west, should not be purchased for residential purposes.

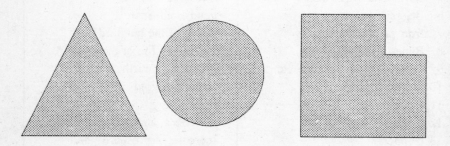

A round house is good for business and trade, but is ominous for residential purposes.

The above picture shows an 'O Shaped' building and another in 'C-Shape' which are good to carry on trade and business, hence quite auspicious, but are inauspicious for residential purposes. It is a view of Missroti town, in America.

India's Parliament House is an O-Shaped, building which is not in comformity with Vaastu rules. Due to this reason, there are unnecessary arguments and feuds (wranglings). No other parliament in the world has witnessed so many unfortunate happenings, feuds and scuffles, altercations which our Parliament has demonstrated.

(III) Segregated and Extended Plots

Q. What would be effects if north-east side of a plot is Segregated?

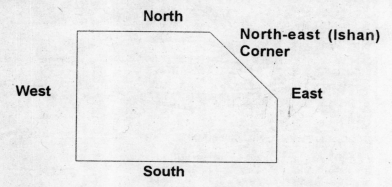

Ans. If north-east direction of a factory is fragmented, paucity of water will always remain there; as water-place exists in the north-east direction.

If north-east direction / corner of a residential plot is cut, its owner will never attain spiritual success. Hence never purchase any plot whose north-east corner is found segregated—it applies equally to factories and houses.

Q. What would be result if north-east side is unholy or unpure?

Ans. According to Vaastu, extremely benefic ultraviolate rays emanate from a building's north-east direction. But, if this corner / direction is sullied, harmful and toxic gases like, carbon dioxide, nitrogen etc. will mix up with oxygen thereby toxifying and spoiling life-giving energy. Due to such developments the plot owner will be impacted by ominous and harmful effects.

Even if all the other directions of a plot are in a favourable situation but, if the north-east is erroneous sullied due to faulty Vaastu, the house or a factory will never progress and prosper. Expenses and income will be on equal footing in such a factory. Even if there are varioius activities, balance sheet of such a factory will be zero. Causes and effects of a sullied and erroneous north-east direction will be as follows:-

Causes	Effects/Results
1 If norht-east corners is higher than other walls.	1. House owner will be subjects to many ill results
2. If north-east corner is erratic, faulty, has cracks, pit or ruins exist.	2. Progeny of the house workers will quarrel owner of factory will be lame and crippled.
3. When a toilet exists in the north-east corner.	3. There will be outgoing wranglings in the house, factory owner will be a moral wreck, will suffer from, various deseases, there will be continuous feuds and loss of money in the family.
4. If there is a heap of debris or rubbish, a heap of waste material and stones.	4. It will cause animosity, lessening of age, and immorality to the house-owner.
5. If broom or mosquito net's rods are kept in the north-east corner.	5. It is a sign of permanent penury.

Q. Which type of the fragmented plots are good or bad?

31

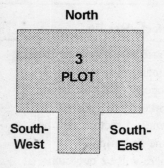

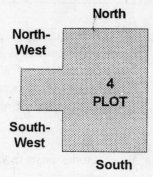

Remarks

1) In this plot of land north-east and north-west sides are fragmented which is not an auspicious sign.

2) Here, in this plot, north-east and east-west corners are fragmented, hence unsuitable.

3) In this plot south-east and south-west corners are fragmented which is an inauspicious sign.

4) In this plot south-west and north-west corners are seen fragmented which is an ominous sign.

Q. On which pathways a house should not extend?

Ans. See the following diagram wherein the house is extending on the southern road, due to which factor it is casting a damaging impact on the western and eastern roads.

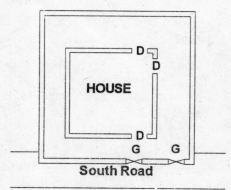

In the following diagram the house is extended towards western road, due to which it is casting bad impact on north side of north-west and south side of south-west direction.

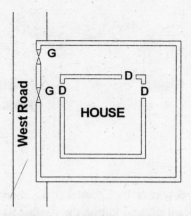

Q. How a house's plot can be tapered or extended?

Ans. Western side of the north-west direction can be extended but it should not extend from south-west to north-west on the plot which has been earmarked for construction—this extension should be to the extent of 6 degress only; and it applies only to the extension face. If north-west side is extended (of a house), then that part becomes heavier and south-west shall weaken which will lose its power. Smilarly, there is no harm if southern part of south-west gets extended, but the house itself should not get extended because it will lose its power, it is extended on the south-west side..

1) See the following figure. If a house is built as shown here-under, its north-east side will get fragmented (cut) which is a fault in Vaastu.

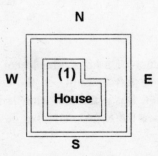

2) If southern part of south-east direction is found fragmented, it is not bad, but the house's southern side on south-east direction should not remain fragmented. If more vacant space is left open on the north-east direction it will constitute a Vaastu fault. If the plot is fragmented on the southern part of south-east direction then plan of the house can be adjusted for house construction.

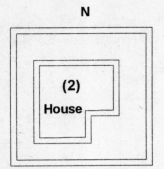

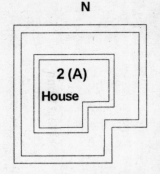

3) If south-west direction is fragmented (cut), then it will constitute a Vaastu fault due to a vacant portion left on the south-east direction. Similarly in addition to the abovesaid factor, if west portion on the north-west direction is left more vacant, it will be another Vaastu fault. Hence a house should never be built, in a fragmented shape, on the south-west direction. But, if the plot itself is pruned on the south-west direction, then house may also be built as per shape of the plot. See the following diagram.

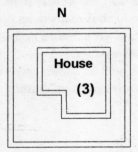

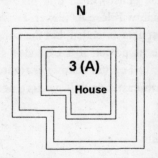

4) North-west direction of a house should not have any cut. If it is so, more vacant area will be left (unbuilt) on the north-east direction which constitutes a Vaastu fault. But if the plot itself is in a pruned shape on the north-west direction, then the house may also be constructed according to shape of the plot.

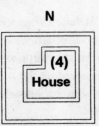

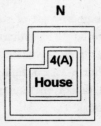

34

Q. How a house should be built when and if the plot of land extends towards south-west, south-east, north-west and north-east directions of the road?

Ans. If north-east side of a plot continues to extend towards, a house can also be built in conformity with shape of the plot. If north-east side extends towards the road on the south-west, then before constructing a house, outer path of the pruned should be sharpened on the south-east direction, but such portion should be left unbuilt. It should be ensured that a house should not extend and intrude into any path or road. Similarly, if portion of a plot extends / intrudes into south portion of south-east direction, western part of south-west direction, western portion of north-west direction or western portion of south-west direction, then such portions should be left out and house constructed on the remaining portion of the plot.

If an eastern road continues to extend towards south-east, then it (plot) should be modified and adjusted as shown in the diagram. Then, in such a situation, each place will extend towards the north-east, but it is beneficial only when only one person is owner of the plot. If it is not so, then north portion of the north-east direction get pruned, which factor will be inauspicious.

If a northern road continues to extend towards northern side of north-west direction, then the house should be built, as shown in the following diagram. In such a situation extension will be towards the north part of north-east direction which is an auspicious sign, but it is possible only when only one man is owner of the plot, otherwise a pruned and tapered north-east portion will prove ominons for the owner of the plot. So, all the said factors should be taken into account while initiating construction of a house on a plot.

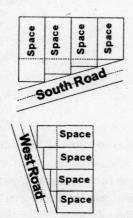

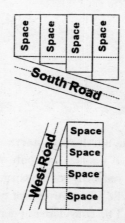

Q. How is that, even if the north-east portion of house is pruned/ cut, the resident are still happy and prosperous?

Ans. When northern portion of north-east direction extends towards a pathway or road, there is more vacant place in the northern side and there is also a slope, then the residents will be affluent and wealthy. But money is not the only be — all and end — all of life, but all things cannot be purchased by money and there are many other factors which are equally important. But a sound sleep, peace of mind, fame etc. cannot be purchased by money. In fact, each direction has its own specific importance and utility. If the north-east side is pruned, it will render a person useless, it can also cast unfavourable impact on health, studies of the children can also be adversely affected, there could also be accidents, their marriage prospects can also be impacted by odds. Hence, if a person has money, even when the north-east direction of his house remains pruned, he cannot be said to be happy, as possession of more wealth, cannot guarantee that everything is in order. What's good of such a wealth if a person is not happy, relaxed, comfortable, does not enjoy sound sleep, does not relish his meals, remains tense and worried. Hence a pruned north-east direction cannot yield auspicious and salutary results, despite good income.

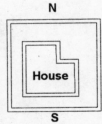

Q. Can north-west, north-east and south-east directions be reduced?

Ans. Of course. But only north-west and south-east directions can be tapered or reduced, but the north-east direction can not be reduced even by an inch's length. If, however, the north-east direction gets extended even by an inch, it will be considered in perfect order. See the following diagrams which depect what has been mentioned here.

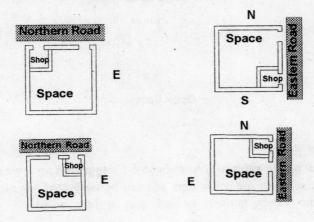

Q. On which directions there should be kept vacant place in a house?

Ans. There should be left more vacant space in a house from west to east and from south to west directions. See the following diagram.

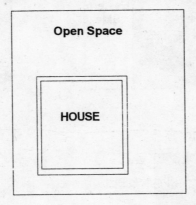

Q. On which sides of the house not much vacant space should be left open?

Ans. Not much vacant space should be left open from north to south and from east to west. It may be noted that if more vacant space is left open in a house on the southern side, then the place, whether a house or a plot, will be disposed of within a span of twelve years.

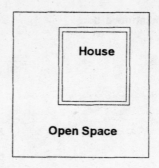

Q. Which of the sides of a house can be integrated or joined?

Ans. The space in the house or a site can be integrated / joined if it is stituated on the eastern, northern or north-eastern direction/site.

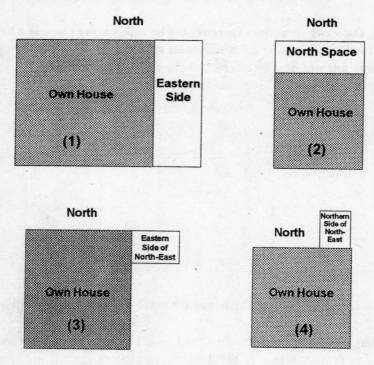

Q. Which of the directions should not be integrated?

Ans. Sites, situated in the north-west, north-east, south-east and south-west directions should not be integrated / joined, as shown in the following diagrams.

38

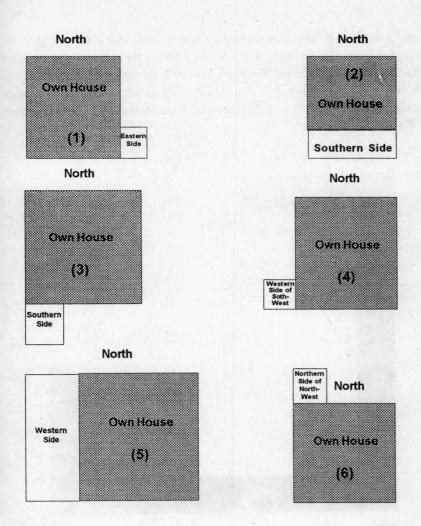

Q. On which directions of the house much weight should not be kept?

Ans. No weighty articles should be kept on the eastern side of south-east direction, on the western side of north-west direction, but on the north side of north-east, not even a straw should be kept.

Q. On which sides can weight be kept?

Ans. The more weight is kept in the rooms that are built on south, west, south-west, south-east, north-west sides, the more beneficial it will be for the comfortable and happy life of the occupant of the house. Remember, any heavy article can be kept alongth the east side of south-east direction, provided it touches the walls. Similarly any heavy article can be kept along the western side of north-west direction. But north part of north-west direction should be left absolutely untouched. But, if it becomes absolutely necessary to keep on the northern side of north-west direction, the material should be stacked slightly of the wall.

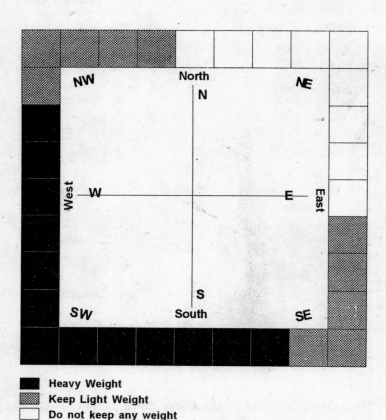

■ Heavy Weight
▨ Keep Light Weight
☐ Do not keep any weight

(IV) Construction work of a building

Q. What the term 'Construction', stand for, in the context of Vaastu?

Ans. Sequence of construction should follow this course — first of all purify and sanctify the land, then walls should be raised. Start digging earth from the north-east direction, while laying down foundation. Foundation-wall should be started from the south-west direction and this portion should be levelled first and then construction work should be started. Before starting construction of the house, carefully examine all the (eight) directions and (four) corners / angles. If there is slope on the east and north side of north-east direction or any pit or a water source, the same should be filled up. Here, no negligence or any lopsided approach is called for. Closely examine the north-east direction and when everything is in order, then dig a well and use this wells water for construction work. Do not pile up or stock construction material (like bricks, stones, iron, steel, cement, sand, wood etc.) on the eastern or northern side, rather stock these items in the western or southern direction. If pillars / poles are necessary, they should be shaped into circular or multi armed arms, using bricks, wood, stones, cement and concrete but pillar on the north-earth direction should necessarily be multi-armed.

Q. In which direction should heavy material be stocked?

Ans. Since south-west direction is considered to be the most suitable site for stocking heavy material, hence it should always be stocked in the said corner.

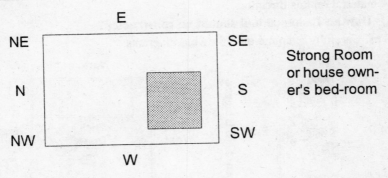

Strong Room or house own-er's bed-room

Q. Where Raw Material should be kept, while building a house?

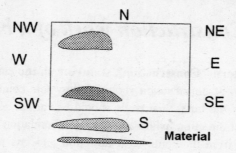

Ans. Before initiating construction of a house, if building material is kept on the north-west or south-west direction, it will help toward rapid construction of a house.

Q. Which of the walls should be high in a house.

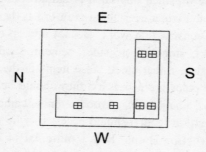

Ans. South-west walls in a house should be comparatively higher in comparison to other walls — it will also confirm justification for keeping heavy material on this direction.

Q. How an L-shaped hall should be constructed?

Ans. Carefully examine the following diagrams.

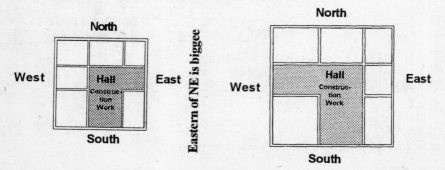

When an 'L-shaped' hall is desired to be built in a house, its eastern side of north-east direction, southern side of south-east direction, western side of north-west direction and northern side of north-west direction should be built in an extended form. But remember, not to let the extensions extend to east of south-east, the south of south-west direction, to the west of south-west direction or to the north of north-west direction.

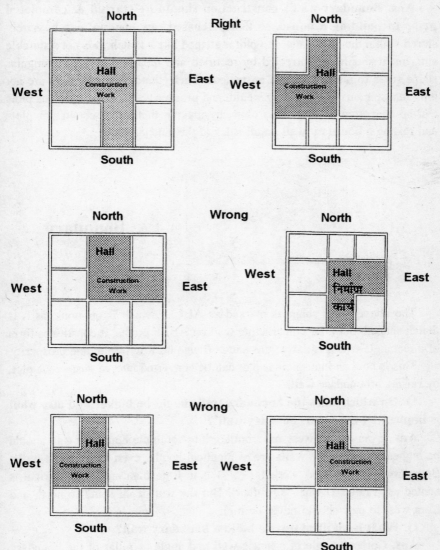

43

(V) Boundary-Wall

Q. Should bounday-wall or house be constructed first?

Ans. Boundary-wall's construction should be started & completed prior to building a house, so that purchased raw material can be safely stored within the four walls. If a plot is shaped like a thatch, it is not a suitable site, but it should be corrected by rectified and modified into a rectangular shape so as to make the same auspicious. Such 'thatch-shaped' plots are not only inauspicious, they destroy wealth and prosperity. Such inauspicious plots can be converted to auspicious plots, by making them into rectangular plots and raising a boundary wall on all sides of the amended plot.

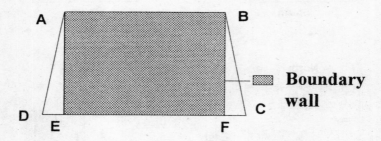

The above plot's shape is marked as ABCD, which is ominous, as it is thatch shaped, but after constructing wall on ABEF points, it constitutes form of a rectangle which is auspicious and will also bestow wealth and prosperity.

This is how an inauspicious plot can be converted into an auspicious plot, by raising a boundary wall.

Q. On which sides the boundary wall should be higher and also what is implied by the term 'bounary wall'?

Ans. From east to west and from north to south the boundary wall should be higher but, if all the walls are of identical height, even then it is in order. Boundary wall is called 'Perkota' (परकोटा) in Rajasthan and in Sanskrit it is named as 'Prahar Diwar' (प्रहर दीवार)! But the wall from south to north and from west to east should never be high.

Q. What is an ideal way to build a boundary wall?

Ans. Corner / angle of a house-wall and angle or pillar of the boundary wall should not be built in the courtyard. No boundary wall should be built in a round or circular shape in the north-east direction. But in other three directions wall can be round or angular (after being rectified) or in whichever it is desired to be built, as it involves no Vaastu fault.

Q. Can creeper of flowers be tagged to the main (entrance) gate or an iron rod?

Ans. Make a semi-circular shaped form on the western and southern gates and then creeper may be tagged to it, as it does not constitute any Vaastu fault. But this rule should not be applied to eastern and western side gates.

Q. What should be the height of a boundary wall?

Ans. The boundary wall of a house can be higher or lower than the height of the main gate, provided such a house has its main gate in the south or west side. But the houses which have main gate in the eastern or northern side, their boundary wall should be lower than the main gate so that the main gate could be seen from the road.

Q. Should the boundary wall or compound be built first?

Ans. If a boundary wall is built first, the space requires for laying foundation may lessen. So, first built a compound. But, if it is not possible to build the entire house, due to any reason whatsoever, then even construction of basement will suffice. Extend north-east direction a bit and build south-west area, then build the boundary wall — it will augur well and also let the Vaastu power fully benefit the house.

Q. Is it not a defect, if boundary wall should remain fallen or unbuilt?

Ans. Boundary wall is constructed to derive fruitful gains, hence it should be fully built or not left midway or remains dismantled. Excepting the north-east side, boundary wall should, at once, be erected on all other directions, otherwise it may prove disadvantageous.

Q. If another person's house is already built to the east and north side of our house, is it necessary to build a boundary wall?

Ans. If another house has been built to the eastern side of your own house, then your eastern direction becomes heavy. Hence, it is necessary to build a boundary wall on the eastern side of your house (where another person's house already exists), leaving a space of three inches from the wall of another person's house.

Following diagrams will clearly explain what has been said heretofore.

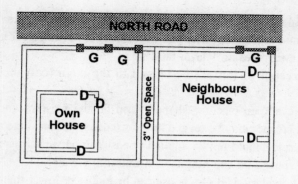

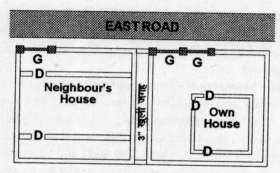

Q. Is it necessary to build compound if the houses exist on the western and southern sides of our house?

Ans. If houses exist on the west and east directions of your house, there is no need to build a verandah but there will also be no harm, if a verandah is built.

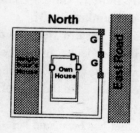

Q. Upon which boundary wall there should not be any construction work?

Ans. No construction work should be done on the Eastern and western walls of the house, because it is not considered auspicious. Similarly, no construction work should be done on the south-east and north-west boundaries of the house.

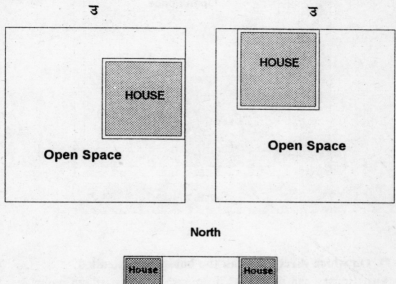

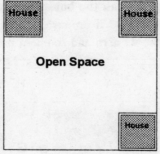

Q. On which boundary construction work yields fruitful results?

Ans. Constructions on south and west boundaries yield favourable results. Construction can still be started, even if there is a road between south and west sides. If plinth of western or southern road is lower tham than your house, then do not build any boundary wall. In such a situation you should leave an area of three feet open from your house, and then build your house. In the same manner if houses of other personss exist on the southern and western sides of your house, even then no house should be built on the boundary wall.

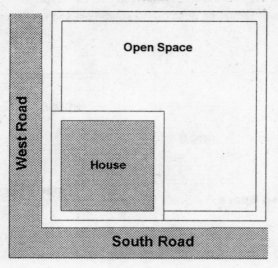

North

Open Space

West Road

House

South Road

Q. On which directions can the houses be extended?

Ans. Houses can be extended on eastern and northern pathways. But extension of houses on the western and southern pathways is not considered auspicious.

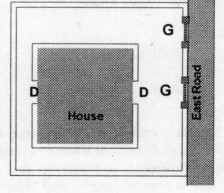

House

G

D   D G

East Road

Remarks : This house is extended towards eastern side's road — it is an auspicious extension, because it will add to area of the house in the direction on north on the north-east direction and towards the south side on south-east direction. Hence, it is in order and fruitful.

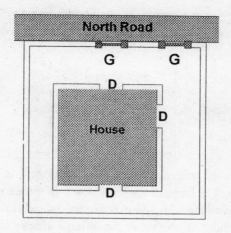

Remarks : This house has extended towards the northern road. It is extending towards the western side of north-west direction and eastern side of the north-east direction, hence this extension is auspicious.

Q. Some people build 2 or 3 houses within one boundary wall, is it in order?

Ans. No, it is not in order, because when two or more houses are built up within a single boundary wall, they lose their power according to Vaastu. See the following diagrams.

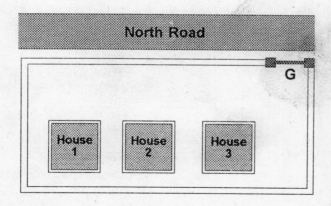

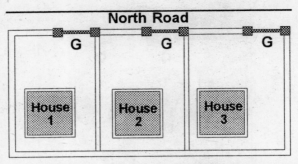

As can be deduced from the first figure, house no-1 is harmful to house no. 2 and house no. 2 is harmful for house no. 3 in the eastern direction. So, it is in the interest of all the house-owners that they should first build separately individual compounds, as shown in the second picture and then build up individual houses — according the Vaastu it will prove auspicious and fruitful.

Q. Should a sub/outhouse be built on the south-west corner of the boundary wall?

Ans. Please see the following diagrams and closely follow the hints given in each diagram.

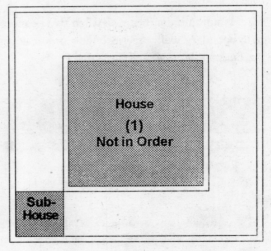

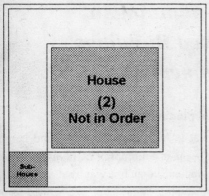

Remarks :-

1. A sub-house should be built which remains attached to the main house.

2. If no pit or water pond (water-tank) exists on either side of the house, then the sub-house can be built separately on the boundary wall.

3. If a water-tank exists outside the house, then the sub-house should be built independent of the house and boundary wall.

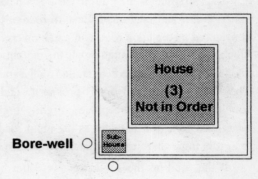

(VI) Door-planning in Multi-storeyed Buildings (Apartments)

Q. Will you guide about the door-planning in apartments?

Ans. In a large piece of land one flat is built upon the other and heigh rises according to the number of flats. — it is a complex of many storeyed flats. So, doors in such flats should be planned in such a way that all the risk parts and cautions should be taken into account. What steps are needed to be adhered to, please closely study and implement the following guidelines.

Such apartments are built in various blocks and each block is an independent entity, that is self contained. Eastern road of the south-east direction should be considered as the main road and a gate is erected on the eastern side of eastern block, which will not augur well for the entire community of dwellers, hence another gate should also be installed on the southern side of south-east direction The southern gate will inpart prosperity and welfare to the inmates, but the southern gate should be placed slightly higher. If the southern road on the south-east direction is taken as the main road and a gate is built on that side then it is imperative to build another gate on the eastern side also.

If the road on the south-west direction is the main road, then it will be appropriate to install a gate on the southern or western side of south-west direction. But if road on the western side of south-west direction is the main road, then the door should be installed on the western side of that direction. If roads exist on both the sides, then gates should not be installed on both the sides and in such a case better of the roads should be deemed as a main road and door installed on that main road only.

In the north-west direction if northern road is taken as the main road, then a gate each should be installed at the northern and eastern sides because, for the residents of the northern wing gate will be a lowly one and for the dwellers in the western wing, it will be high gate.

It is imperative for the residents of north-east direction to install a gate at the eastern side of north-east directon.

52

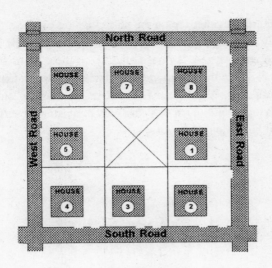

Q. Which directions are considered auspiciouis and good when a door is to be installed in the boundary-wall according to Vaastu principles.

Ans. According to Vaastu principles east, southern side of south-east direction, western side of the north-west direction, northern side of north-east direction are said to be the most suitable and appropriate venues where a gate should be installed in the boundary-wall.

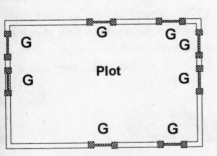

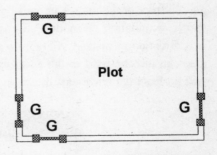

Q. Which are the directions where installation of a gate is prohibited?

Ans. No gate should ever be installed in the eastern part of south-east direction, southern part of south-west direction, western side of south-west direction and northern part of north-west direction.

Q. How should a gate be built towards the road side on the eastern side?

Ans. If a house is built in south-west direction as per Vaastu rules and there is also more vacant space on the north than on south portion and if a gate is built exactly in front of the main-gate, then the gate will be lowly. Similarly, if the plinth of another gate is raised slightly on the eastern side of north-east direction it will dispel the Vaastu defect which is quite evident in the previous position. In addition, a gate can be built on the eastern side of north-east direction, on a higher plinth (in this case only one gate will suffice) and the exit and entry will be through this gate only.

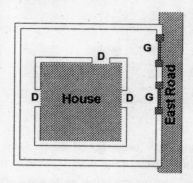

Q. How do you suggest installation of a gate (if the house is built in the south-west direction) towards a road on the northern side?

Ans. If gate of the boundary wall lies opposite to the main gate, and there is also more vacant area in the east than the west side, then, in such a situation, gate in front of the main gate will be in a lowly place. To ward of this Vaastu defect, installation of another gate is required on the northern side of north-east direction or instead of erecting a gate in front of the main gate, another gate can also be built in the north-east direction. In this case, entry and exit will be from the north-east direction only.

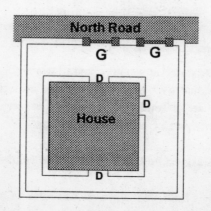

Q. Where should the gate be built, if a house is built on the southern side of south-west direction?

Ans. If boundary wall is opposite the main-gate and there is more vacant area in the east than in the western portion and the southern side is also lowly, it becomes necessary to instal another gate on the south side of south-east direction. So, only one gate will not suffice. There is, however, no harm if only a single gate is erected, on a higher padestal, in front of the main gate.

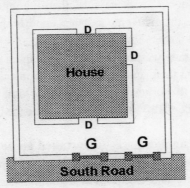

Q. What is the method to instal a gate on the western side of south-west direction?

Ans. First instal a gate in front of main gate of the house, then instal another gate (on the vacant area) between the boundary wall and the first gate. So, only one gate should not be installed in such a house. But, if only a single gate is built on a higher plinth (infront of the main gate) there is no need to erect another gate.

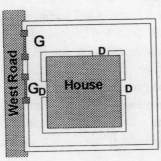

Q. How a smaller gate be installed in the main gate of a house?

Ans. It is a common practice to erect a gate in the boundary wall. Such a gate is generally opened when some function is to be celebrated (like marriage, birthday parties etc.). But a smaller gate is also made so that all the entrants pass through it in routine course.

If main entrance gate is on the eastern side, then gate should be erected on a higher plinth and the smaller gate should be erected on the northern side of this gate and if exit and entry is through the north-east directions, it is an excellent situation. If the gate is on the southern side, it will cast bad impact.

If the house is facing southern side, then the gate should be erected on higher plinth opposite the main gate and then another small gate should be built thereafter — it is an auspicious proposition.

If the house is facing western direction, then main gate should be installed on a higher plinth and then small gate should be installed oppisite the gate of boundary wall. It will be an auspicious proposition. If the smaller gate is installed in accordance with Vaastu rules, it will be the beginning of good times automatically.

Q. How should smaller gates be installed on both sides of the house?

Ans. People instal small gates, in the small lane which is adjacent to the house for routine entry and exit. If it is done, no Vaastu fault is involved in doing so, but it requires adherance to certain established norms.

It has generally been observed that people build smaller gates, on the southern side of south-east direction and the northern side of north-east direction (it applies to those houses which are east facing) in the backyard of the house, for entry and exit. But, at times, Vaastu defects creep in while installing such gates in the boundary wall. It is harmful also, because the defect arises due to southern gate. Though entry and exit through northern gate is in order, but it (gate) should not be adjacent to the house and boundary wall. Vaastu faults can be removed if too much space is left vacant in between the house and the boundary wall, erect a wall there and then instal the gate. These norms apply equally in the case of southern direction also.

If a house is south-facing, then small gates should be built on the western side of south-east direction (towards sides of the house). But, from the eastern gate south side of south-east direction and western side of south-west direction will prove harmful. In such a situation, if erection of a door is necessary, then occupants should leave a space of two inches vacant between the boundary wall and the house and then build a wall.

It is not proper to erect small gate on the sides of a west facing house on the northern side of north-west direction and southern side of south-west direction in the boundary wall. Northern gate is considerd auspicious but western

56

gate will prove ominous. If it is felt necessary to erect such type of gate, leave a gap of two inches between the boundary wall and walls of the house and then erect a gate, as it will help to dispel Vaastu faults, thereby proving auspicious.

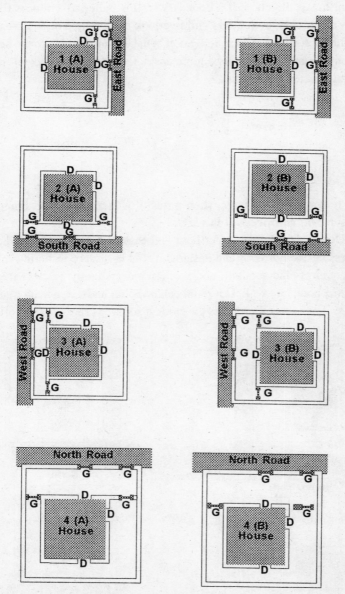

Q. How a gate should be erected when eastern and northern sides of north-east directions are found extended & towards the boundary wall?

Ans. If eastern and northern corners of roads continue to extend on each sides of the road, then the extension will be towards northern and eastern sides of north-east direction. If a boundary wall is built and a door is fixed on erected on either side, both doors will overlook eastern side of south-east and northern side of north-west direction. So, if equal distance is mantained between ends of both the gates, they will be more auspicious, as they will point towards northern and eastern directions.

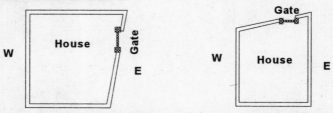

Q. Is it not a Vaastu fault when gates of a factory are designed on a new pattern and compressed inwards?

Ans. Doors of a factory in northern and eastern sides should not be built by compressing the northern and eastern. If it is necessary to build such type of gates, compress the southern and western sides slightly or erect the gates parallel to the boundary wall. Our point can be better understood and translated into practise if one carefully studies the guiding points, as shown in the following diagrams.

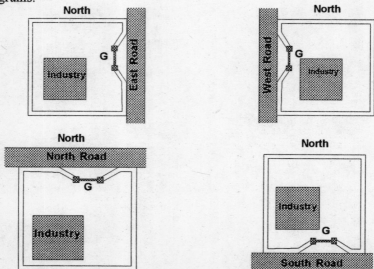

(VII) Place of Water-source in a Plot

Q. Which are the ideal sites in a plot where arrangement for water-source should me made?

Ans. An ideal situation for digging a well or making a water-storage (reservoir) is west, east, north and corner of north-east direction, as these are the auspicious sites for the purpose, moreover these are the places of Varun, Lord of Water. But no well / water reservoir should ever be south-east, south-west, north-west or southern sides.

Q. What effects will be cast if a water-resource is provided in the above mentioned, central and other parts of the house?

Ans. Following comparative description will clearly spell out the plus and minus points, if a well or water-reserviur is provided for in a specific side.

	Side and directions	Effects
1.	North-east, north, east and west	Auspicious
2.	South-west corner	Loss of Son
3.	South	Loss of wife
4.	North-West	Tormentation by enemy
5.	Centre of the house	Loss of accumulated money

Q. Which are the ideal sites in a plot of land where well and other sources of water could be built and what are the benefits?

Ans. Well in a house, swimming pool, well in an agricultural field, and well in a commercial complex, other water resources/reservoirs / tanks should be provided for in the following sites and the benefits will accrue as follows :-

	Direction	Benefits
1.	North-east corner	House-owner's family remains prosperous and happy
2.	West	Increase in prosperity and wealth.
3.	East	Increase in comforts & luxuries
4.	North	Increase in comforts, peace and tranquality.

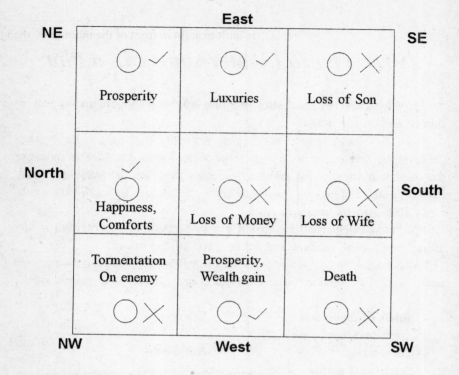

The above description is a clear guide to your question.

Q. Which are the auspicious Nakhshastras (Asterism, Constellations) for digging a well & in a plot of land?

Ans. It has been mentioned—

"पुष्ये हस्ते डबुभं तोयेऽलुराधे वासवे धृते।

पौष्णे मधायां च मृगे कूपारम्भः शुभः स्मृतः॥

[Pushaye Hastey Ambhubhey, Toye Anuvaethey Vaaswey Dhretey, Paushane Maghayain Cha Mrigey Kooparambhah Shubhah Smritey.—

That is the auspiciouis time for starting digging of a well is fruitful if the well is dug up in Pushya, Hasta, Swatbhisha, Poorvashadha, Anuradva, Dhanishtha, Uttrashdha, Uttraphalguni, Uttra Bhadrapada, Rohini, Revati, Magha and Mrigshira Asterism.

Q. Which are the auspicious months for digging a well?

Ans. Phalgun, Magha, Agahan, Jyestha, Kartik and Vaishakh months (of Vikrami Samvat) are the auspicious months for digging a well.

Q. What is the significance of an auspicioius inauguration in digging a well?

Ans. If any work is done in an auspicious occasion, it yields success. Heavenly powers get pleaseed if rules of nature are followed and they also help to impact success to the initiated work.

Q. How a water-pond or boring should be constructed in a house?

Ans. As a rule no water-pond or boring should be affected on the north-east direction of a house. Draw a line, with the help of a rope, from the north-east corner to the boundary wall and then dig earth for building a water-pond on either side of the drawn line. But take care that such a water-pond should exist on the north-east area only. If more space is available in the northern side, then water-pond may be built up in the north side of north-east direction or when more space is available on the east side, earth should be dug up on the eastern side for constructing a water-pond.

Q. Which type of roof should be built over a Pumpset?

Ans. If a Pumpset is installed in the north-east direction and roof is also provided above it, the roof should not be slopy and it should also not touch the adjacent wall. Moreover, a well or a water-pond should not touch the boundary wall, that is there must be a gap between the two.

Q. Why no square structure should be built over a water-pond?

Ans. If any squarish structure is erected over a water-pond, it will constitute intrudence of an angle or a corner, hence it is not proper.

Q. What type of platforms are in order around a water-pond?

Ans. Platforms around a water pond should be of such a type which should be below the level of the house, camaflouge and south-west direction. Further, such platforms should also not touch the northern and eastern walls.

Q. Do some other directions also exist where water-tank should be built?

Ans. Certainly, if it is not possible to make water-pond in the north-east direction, it can be made in the eastern or northern side of this direction.

The following diagram will clearly explain our viewpoint.

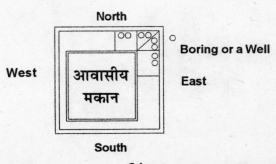

Q. Which are the ideal days (dates) to start inaugural digging of a well?

Ans. तृतीयाऽष्टमी सप्तमी कामतिथ्ययम्।

दशम्यां हि, तोया शयारम्भ श्रेष्ठम्॥

Tritiyaashtami, Saptami Kamtithyam, Dashamayaam Hi, Toyashyarambha Shreshtham

That means that for the inauguration of well digging 3rd, 7th, 8th, 10th, 13th days are the most ideal and auspicious days for the purpose.

Q. Which are the most auspicious days recommended for digging a well?

Ans.

चन्द्रे सोम सुते वारे तथा वाचस्पतेर्दिन।

कूपदे खननं क्रूरे शुक्रे न शोभनम्॥

[Chandrey some sutey Varey, Tatha Vachaspateyerdinam,

Koopadey Khananam Kroorey Shukrey Na Shobnam]

According to the said couplet, any monday, wednesday and thursday are the most auspicious days to start earth-digging to dig a well. But do not do so on any friday and tuesday, as these are the ominous days for digging a well.

Q. Which are the auspicious ascendants eulogised for starting earth digging for a well?

Ans. Though all the ascendants are considered auspicous for well digging, yet the most auspicious ascendents are those whose trait is water dominated and also that the moon is also posited in that ascendant. But well-digging is inauspicious in Leo, Scorpion and Sagittarius ascendants.

Q. On which sides of a boundary-wall a water tank should not be built or dug up?

North

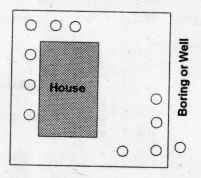

62

Ans. No pit should be dug up in the eastern side of north-east direction, for the purposes of building a well or boring. Similarly, there should also be no water pond on the southern side of south-east direction or this direction itself. Existence of any water pond on the southern side of south-west direction and western side of north-west direction cause incalculable and horrible damages. Similarly if a pit is dug up to built a water-pond on the western side of north-west direction, it is also inauspicious.

Q. If it is not possible to dig a water-pond in a field, which is the other option?

Ans. In case it is not possible to provide for a water-pond on the north-east direction of a field, it can be provided for in the south-west, north-west or north-east directions, but there must also be a big tree on the south-west direction of the water-pond. Also ensure that north-east corner of the tree should also be away from the water-pond. Well, meant to fetch water, should be towards the north - south directions.

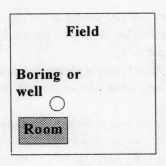

Q. If a water-pond or boring exists to the right or left side of the house, how should it be filled?

Ans. If any useless (unused) pit or water-pond exists around any place of a house, it should be levelled and filled. Some people use stone-slabs, cement-slabs or bamboo slices for filling purposes, but it is wrong, as it fails to serve the desired purpose. Water-pond or a pit should be first filled in with dust or sand, then cement or stones should be put thereon,. It should be opened after sometime and refilled with sand, because with passage of time the filled in material sinks. It should be properly levelled and then sealed with cement slab or a stone.

Overhead Tank

Q. Which is the ideal site for an overhead tank in a house?

Ans. It can be built in the north-west and south-west directions.

Q. If an overhead tank can only be built in the south-west or north-west direction, then what corrective measures need to be taken?

Ans. Build a small room in the south-west direction, and its height should be equal to height of the overhead water-tank.

Q. If we wish to erect an overhead tank in the north-west direction, will it pose any problems?

Ans. There is no Vaastu fault involved here, hence you can well proceed. If an overhead tank is built in this direction, there is no need for constructing any extra room or structure.

Q. We have heard that it is prohibited to build an overhead tank in the north-west, south-east and north-west directions, then what should be done?

Ans. Yes, no water should be stored in the pits on the said directions, but an overhead water tank can be built over the top of house but it must be of stone slabs or a synthetic tank.

Q. North-east is (divine) godly place and ganges also emanates from Lord Shiva's head. Then what will happen, if an overhead tank is built on this direction?

Ans. These are ancient and useless conclusious and are not backed by any sound reasoning. Such remarks are made by only those people who fail to understand importance of north-east direction. I have seen many people suffering due to building overhead tanks in this direction, hence it is not considered in order.

Q. If there is no other option but to build an overhead tank in the north-east direction, then which steps are required to be taken?

Ans. In such a situation a higher construction than the overhead tank in the north-west direction and a higher construction in the south-east direction than the north-west direction and still higher construction than the north-east direction than the construction in the south-west direction must be ensured, but follow completely the above mentioned sequence.

Q. Can a tank be made in the ground on a north-east direction?

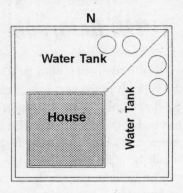

Ans. A tank should be built in the underground area of south-east direction. If a tank is built upon the ground, it should be ensured that the same does not touch the east and north directions. Moreover, level (plinth) of the tank should be lower than the level of the ground.

Q. Which is an ideal place for an overhead tank in a house?

Ans. Place for storing water in a house is north-east (Ishaan) angle. According to this theory a water tank should be built in this direction only. But if an overhead tank is built towards the said site, its height will exceed height of the house and it will cause overburdening of this side with greater weight, which is not considered in order. According to Vaastu principles, a north-east corner of a house should be wide open and light and south-west corner should be heavy and higher. Hence an ideal and most suitable site for an overhead tank is (corner of) the south-west direction.

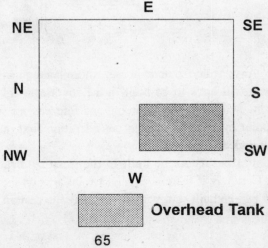

(VIII) Bathroom

Q. In which direction a bathroom would be ideal in a house?

Ans. Bathrooms can be built in the northern or eastern room of a house.

Q. What should be direction of a bathroom in the bedroom?

Ans. A bathroom can be built in the east or west side of a bedroom. There is also no harm if a bathroom is built in the northern side of one room and another in the southern side of other room.

Q. Can a bathroom be built in the north-east direction of a room?

Ans. If the north-eastern side is not covered, a bathroom can be built in the house, but do not have any stove/hearth in that room. But, you can install a heater or boiler in such a room, but such articles should be kept in the south-east direction only.

Q. Can a bathroom be built in the courtyard of a house, main gate faces eastern side?

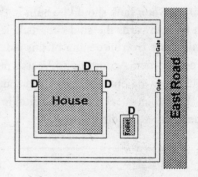

Ans. Away from the main house, whose main gate is facing eastern side, a bathroom will have to be built in the south-east side. The vacant place, between the house and the bathroom and four eastern walls should be more — this point must be taken into consideration first, and then construction should be undertaken.

Q. Can a bathroom be built in the western direction of the house?

Ans. Certainly if there is enough vacant area on the western side, then a bathroom can be built (but without touching the eastern boundary wall). But the plinth level of the bathroom should be slightly higher in comparison to the flooring level of the house. In this case door of the bathroom should be on the northern side, as shown in the following diagram.

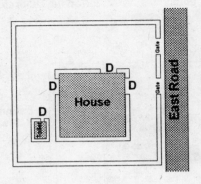

Q. What should be the position of a bathroom in a house whose main-gate is facing south side?

Ans. The bathroom should be built (on the north side of north-west direction) but without touching the main house and the boundary wall. But, it must be ensured the vacant place between the bathroom and boundary wall should be more than the vacant area between house and bathroom. Door of the bathroom should open towards the eastern side, as shown in the following diagram.

Q. What should be the position of a bathroom in a house whose main-gate is facing the western side?

Ans. If you desire to build a bathroom in the backyard of the house, then proceed as suggested in the case of a south facing main-gate. If you want to build a bathroom in the north, then proceed as suggested in the case of a house whose main-gate is facing the south direction. This solution also applies to the house whose main-gate is facing the north side.

Q. Where should the washerman's stone be installed?

Ans. Follow the guidelines of the following diagram.

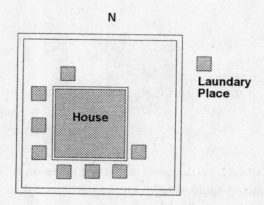

Q. Where the boiler for hot water be installed in a house?

Ans. See the following diagram and proceed as shown in the diagram.

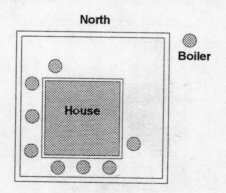

(IX) Toilet and Septic Tank

Q. On which side a latrine and septic tank should be built in a east-facing house?

Ans. If the neighbouring house is glued to the southern wall; latrine should be built alongside the southern wall or else latrine should be built alongside the boundary. But a pit or septic pit should always be dug up along the length of eastern wall.

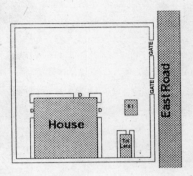

Q. On which direction septic tank should be built?

Ans. Septic tank should be built in the midway of north direction but without touching the house and the compound. In the same manner septic tank can also be built in the eastern direction, other conditions remaining the same.

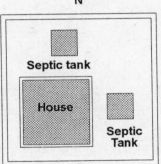

Q. Can a toilet be built in the south-west direction?

Ans. If a toilet is built without a pit, there is no Vaastu fault involved but these days septic latrine is built alongwith a pit which is a wrong method. If it is absolutely necessary to build a latrine in the south-west direction, then it should be built on a higher plinth, but without digging a pit. If digging of pit is a necessity, a pit should be dug up in the midway along the northern length, it can be dug up in the midway to eastern length.

Q. How a latrine should be built in the north-west direction?

Ans. If western wall of the house is separate from it, then a latrine can be built but it should not touch northern wall and boundary wall. That is, the latrine should be built in such a way that it touches the western wall . Here also a pit should be dug up in the high portion of northern side.

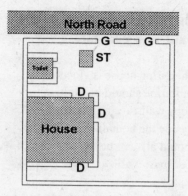

Q. Where and in which direction the basin (commode of the latrine) should be fixed/built?

Ans. It should be in the north or southern direction, but the sitting person's face should be towards the north or south direction.

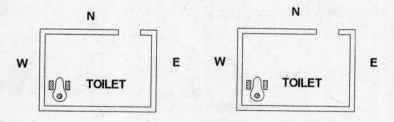

In Srimad Ramayana Bharat said that 'Am I a fool that I will discharge faeces while by keeping my face towards the rising Sun or keep my back towards the Sun?' These words he uttered when he tried to offset baseless disrepute heaped upon him.

Q. In which room of a house can bathroom and latrine be built?

Ans. Study the following diagram.

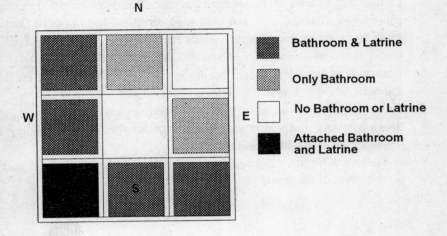

Q. Which is an appropriately suitable place for a toilet in a house?

Ans. Exact place for toilet in a house should be as shown in the following diagram, but there are also relevant norms & rules which should also be followed.

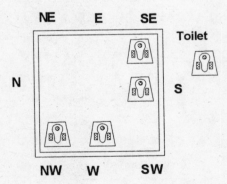

Relevant rules in this regard are summed up as under which need to be observed while planning to construct a latrine in a plot of land, Viz.

1. Toilet should not exist in the western or southern directions.
2. Toilet and kitchen should never be face to face with each other, that is doors of both should not be opposite each other.
3. If bathroom and toilet are built combined at a place, then make sure that

71

seat or commode are not built on the eastern on south east direction.

4. While sitting in a latrine, the sitting person's face should be towards the east, so that he does not suffer from gas, constipation and warts. His face can also be towards north and north-east direction, but never sit facing south and west as it can cause various diseases.

5. Doors of the toilet should open towards the east.

6. Commode in the toilet should be in the south-west direction or on the southern side which is a still better position.

7. Toilet can also be built in south-west or south direction.

8. South-east and north-west are good directions for fixing / building a commode or else central portion of west.

9. In a large and lengthy building, no toilet should be built at the starting point or end-point of the house.

(X) OBSTACLES (VEDHA)

Q. What is meant by VEDHA?

Ans. This term is applied to express the obstacles faced in the free flow of sunrays and wind into a house and it is important aspect of Indian architecture. 'Vedha' is a technical term which has many connotations, as it is not only applicable to various facets of a house, but it also compasses various places, entries and other conditions which are necessary in the context of a house.

No such faults should be allowed to surface in the houses and buildings which are commonly built in the urban areas. These obstacles should be warded off, as far as possible, so that the problems, caused by such obstacles, do not create any problems to the dwellers in such buildings / houses.

Q. What are the types of 'Vedhas'?

Ans. According to Vaastu science treatises, general type of 'Vedhas' have also been mentioned and there are of seven types, viz 'Tal Vedha (तालवेध), 'Taalu Vedha' (तालूवेध), 'Kalaa Vedha' (कलावेध), 'Stambha Vedha' (स्तंभवेध), 'Tulaa Vedha' (तुलावेध), 'Kona Vedha' (कोणवेध) and 'Dwaar Vedha' (द्वारवेध)

The said types of obstacles (Vedhas) are based upon ancient parametres and standards, but according to our experience there are as many as 54 types of 'Vedhas'. Here we will throw light on all the ancient and modern types of 'Vedhas' in considerable details.

Q. What is meant by 'Naabhi Vedha' (नाभिवेध)?

Ans. Whenever plot of land is dug up to build a house, we first of all try to ascertain whether this type of 'Vedha' exists or not. Only Lord Shankar's temple should be built opposite another temple of Lord Shankar and no temple of any other deity should ever be built. If this condition is not complied well, constitute 'Naabhi Vedha'. Similarly temples of Brahma, Vishnu, and venerable person and Lord Surya (Sun) should have only the temples of the said dijties opposite their temples. No Nabhi 'Vedha' is involved if Brahma's temple lies opposite Vishnu's temple, but this exception does not apply in other cases. If this type of obstacle exists in a house, it will cause many problems to the house-owner and the architect - this is with reference to temples only.

In case of houses and buildings, it has been maintained that no building should exist in the back portion of Lord Mahavir of the Jains. It is also not proper to build any building on the sides of temples of Shanker and Surya. There should not also exist any house, any building on the sides of temples of Vishnu and Brahma. In the case of Goddess Chandy, there should not be built any building in the front, back portions and sides of the temple's building, or even in the neighbourhood. But a building can be built and there will not be any 'Naabhi Vedha, if there is a national highway or two walls and / or there is a difference of height between the two buildings (that is, height of one building should be double the height of another building) — in such conditions, 'Naabhi Vedha' does not apply.

Q. What is implied by the term 'Tal Vedha, (तलवेध)?

Ans. 'Talvedha' defect is of 5 kinds, Viz.

i) If the level of doors of a house is not at level.

ii) Doors, windows, nets etc. are in a level - this consideration still exists, as it is neacessary condition for providing sturdity to a house.

iii) When the centre-point or verandah of a house is higher when compared to basic plinth of the house. This condition is necessary in the context of cosmetic appearance of a house, because 'Garbha-Griha' of a house should look elevated.

iv) If plot of a house is not at level, but is uneven. Even these days the elevated portion of land is tapered, if two much variation exists between low and high lands or earth is filled in the lower part of land, so as to make it parallel to the elevated portion.

v) If the land is inclined (bent) towards the southern side.

Q. What is meant by 'Taalu-Vedha' (तालु–वेध)?

Ans. This obstacle occurs when beams / girders are not at level and also the seat in room.

Q. What is meant by 'Tula-Vedha' (तुला–वेध)?

Ans. This obstacle is of 3 types, Viz. i) When beams or pillars are not at level ii) When one beam lies at right angel to another beam, but there is no pillar. If both the beams lie at right angle position, then weight of a house is much greater, hence if there are no pillars, the beams will not be able to withstand such a heavy weight iii) Beams of upper storeys are not according to standard measurements. If a beam measures less than the required weight, it would be impossible for them to sustain and bear the weight. If the beams are heavier than the required weight, they have to bear extra weight and it will unbalance their weight bearing capacity. Hence, this type of Vedha should not be allowed to exist.

Q. What is a Kona-Vedha (कोण–वेध)?

Ans. This type of obstacle occurs when corner of another house exists in front of the main / entrance gate of another house.

Q. What is meant by 'Kapaal-Vedha' (कपाल–वेध)?

Ans. It means when a beam is built / fixed at the central or any other portion of a door. Doors and windows in any house are the weaker points in a house, hence weight of a beam must be borne by a pillar and not window or door. So, this type of defect implies absence of a pillar to support a beam.

Q. What is implied by 'Stambha Vedha' (स्तम्भ–वेध)?

Ans. It is of five kinds, as detailed hereunder.

i) When thickness of pillars, erected in a row, is at variance that is it is less or more.

ii) When all the pillars not in one line.

iii) When a pillar exists opposite windows and doors.

iv) If a pillar exists at the sensitive and weak sites of a house.

v) When a pillar exists at the central part of a house.

All the relevant rules have been framed so that weight falls not only on one pillar but equally shared by other pillars also. If only a pillar is built at the centre point of a house, it is neither convenient nor cost effective, nor it will be so strong as to bear weight of the entire house or building, hence do not let this type of obstacle surface.

Q. What is meant by 'Dwaar-Vedha' (द्वार–वेध)?

Ans. It means any obstructing factor in front of the extrance gate. It is caused by five factors such as :

i) If no storeyes are built on a house, then do not keep a door on the back side.

ii) When the foundation stone of a door is uneven.

iii) There should be no crossing, small or big well, big gutter, corner of another house, big tree, number of poles, drive way, big chariot or a peg to tie the animals in front of entry gate of a house or building.

iv) There should also not be any lane or path in front of the entrance gate. It may also be noted that, if anyone of the obstructive situations exist in front of an entrance gate, the safety of the house will be threatened and endangered. Further, any person can mix up with the crowd at the crossing, after killing the house owner. Any person can hide himself behind the small or big well, wall or corner of another house or behind the animals and kill the house-owner. Hence 'Dwaar Vedha' is detrimental.

v) There should be no marsh or flowing water in front of the entrance

75

gate. If either of these things exists permanently, it will raise the level of earth and thus weaken foundation of the house, hence it is also called as 'Dwaar Vedha'. According to ancient scholars, there are 8 Kinds of 'Dwaar Vedha', such as :

1) **Swar-Vedha** (स्वर–वेध)

When the doors of the house creak and create a creaking sound while being opened or shut.

2) **Keel-Vedha** (कील–वेध)

Existence of Pegs, in front of the house, to tie cows or any other animals to them.

3) Do not build / erect any door at the centre or joining point of a house.

4) Do not construct any door at the backside of the house, if the same has no storey upon it.

5) When it is advised that there should be not pathway (drive way), cross, well, pond, gutter, corner of another house, big tree or pole, pegs to tie the animals, garrage etc. the motive to ensure safety of the house and its inmates.

6) There should not exist any filth, marsh or flowing water in front of a house, as it weakens foundation of the house, that is why it has been nomenclated as 'Dwaarvedha'.

7) **Koopa-Vedha** (कूप–वेध) There should be no well, main hole, water reservior, water tank in front of any house. If shadow of a tank or house falls on the well, it constitutes 'Koopa Vedha'.

8. **Bhrama-Vedha** (ब्रह्मवेध)

If an oil expeller or gutter exists in front of the entrance gate of a house, it constitutes 'Bhrama Vedha' — it creates many tormenting problems.

If there is any big wall, 'compound wall' big holder or any other obstacle, it constitutes 'Dwaar-Vedha', which proves a hurdle to house owner's prosperity and progress.

You can see in diagram no. (2) that the compound wall of the factory is perfectly in order but gate of the boundary wall is bigger than the main gate and the boundary wall itself — such type of constructions scuttle and impede fortunes of the house owner and also destroy the entire industrial enterprise. So, always keep in mind that gate of the boundary wall should never be higher than the main gate and the gate of the boundary wall.

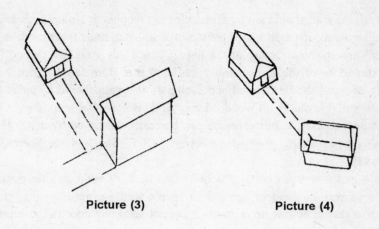

| Picture (3) | Picture (4) |

See figures (3) and (4) Wall of another house should lie in front a house, meant for own residential purposes, otherwise it will stop progress of the house owner.

Q. Have the merits and demerits of doors, also been discussed in Vaastu science?

Ans. Of course, these fausts have all been discussed at length in Vaastu science; the relevant details thereof are being mentioned here under:-

Entrance gate of a house should not exist in the central part. It should not be on one side also, but, at the same time, it should not exist on the corner also.

Actually house construction depends upon the entrance gate of a house. If an entrance door exists in the centre / front of a house, it is called 'Utsang'. Which is ominous for the house owner, as it can cause his death. Hence such a door and its (said) location does not augur well for the house owner. While entering the house if the entrance gate is built in such a place, where the house lies to the right side, such a house is termed as 'Heenbaahuk' which is condemned by the architects, because the person, living in such a house, always feels absence/derth of money, friends and relatives, in addition he remains ill also. But, if the entrance gate is situated at such a venue where house lies to the right side, it is called us 'Poornabahuk', as such a door is auspicious. If a gate exists at the back side also, it is also called Heena Baahuk'. Which is also on ominous position for the house owner (Ref. Samraangan Sootraadhar, 39, 11-17)

No two doors be in front of each other in a house. If a door already exists

77

in a wall, the wall should not be dismantled to erect another gate. Existence of a gate weakens strength of a house and if another door is erected, it will further weaken the structure of the house; hence this guideline. Wood for a door should be of the same quality and also free from termite, hence best quality of wood should be used and each part of a gate should be made from the most suitable quality of wood. Mango wood is not suitable for the doors as it contracts quickly, is unstable and can be easily destoryed by moth. Hence use only the best quality of wood to erect doors (Ref. : Samaraangan Sootraadhar 39,40-41)

In a multi-storeyed house a door should be built upon another door. Do not erect a wall on the door, nor a door upon a wall. i.e. gates for entry to the stair case should be one upon another. Do not keep any door in the centre of house nor even on the 'step'.

Even if a house is multistoreyed, its front entrance and back entrance gate should not face each, so that the back-door is not visible through the front gate. Do not build any gate in both the back sides of the house Ref. Samraangan Sootradhaar 39, 44-59).

Fix doors in the walls nicely and suitably prune and chisel all the corners so that they are identical from all the sides. Doors should be in rectangular shape. All doors should be uncurved, unbent or unconstricted. They should be parallel to the wall, neither too high nor too wide, that is length and breadth should have identical thickness, height and width. A door should not be equal in width to the width of the wall at the centre part, but none of its portions should exceed width of a wall. (S. Sootradhaar, 39.35-38).

Doors of a gate should not open and shut automatically nor should there be any creaking voice while opening and shutting the doors Ref. : S. Sootraadhr (48.73-74)

Q. What is meant by 'Maarg-Vedha' (मार्ग—वेध)?

Ans. If a path or lane is situated in front of main entrance gate of a house, such a gate is an open invitation for theft, as thieves can enter in such a house with almost ease. Secondly, any passer by can also peep into the house. If there is only one way for entry and exit and there is also a common entry point

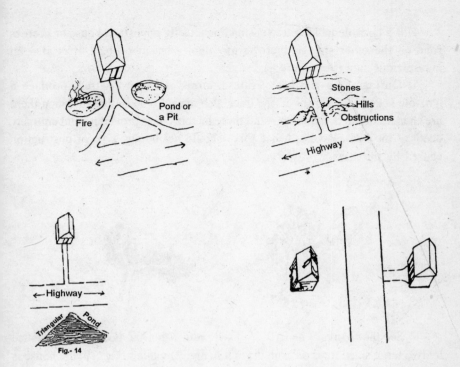

Fig.- 14

for entrance, it will provide a safety to the dwellers and the house owners.

If a ruin exists in front of a house and a person sees such a spectre daily, his fall and degredation is certain, his industry trade and profession will also be afflicted, resulting a slide down and an ultimate end to his occupation.

Q. What is the import of 'Vrikhsha Vedha' (वृक्ष–वेध)?

Ans. If a big tree is situated in front of the main entrance of a house, it is known as 'Vrikhsha-Vedha', It is said older the tree, older its age. If such a big tree falls upon a house, it will do spell disaster for that house and its demerits are detailed here under:-

1) If a tree exists in the immediate vicinity of a house, it will weakan foundation and also cause cracks in the walls of a house.

2) Different types of animals and birds sit under or upon such a tree, leaves of tree fall in the house, due to which there is great possibility of harm to persons and material in the house.

3) No dry / barren tree or a stem should exist opposite the door, as its presence forebodes inauspicious effects. Shadow of such a tree should not fall upon the house, as this obstruction, cost by a tree, is ominous (See figure,9).

4) If a horrible looking tree is standing exactly opposite a house or accross road on the other side or there is any dual - branched tree, it is also an inauspicious sign (See figure 8).

5) During sharp and heavy rains, storms and typhoon trees produce a horrible sound. Further, high rise trees also attract clouds, due to which there are chances of fall of lightning — all these factors cause premature and untimely death of the house owner; hence there should not be any type of obstruction caused by the trees.

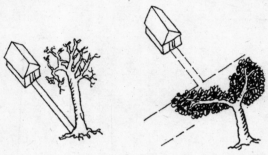

6) See the figures 9 and 10. You will notice that the house is surrounded by two large sized trees on both the sides (Fig. 9) while in fig. 10, the house is surrounded three large trees. Such secluded sites or houses may serve the purpose of ascetics, realised persons, yogis and saints, but such houses are inauspicious for a family person.

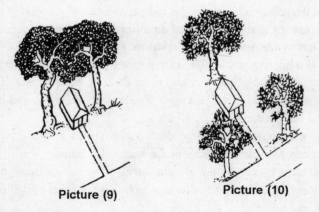

Picture (9)   Picture (10)

7) As a rule, shadow of any tree should not fall on any building, house or factory for more than three hours. Similarly, when shadow of a tree is on its last lap (of three hours), such a shadow's fall on any house is not auspicious.

Meaning : 8) It is also another type of 'Vriksha-Vedha' when prohibited trees are planted at the entrance gate and / or all arround. For instance, 'Udumbar' tree should not be planted in the east direction, Banyan tree in the southern direction and 'Nyodhra' tree in the western direction.

9) Any type of a fruit tree, a tree from which milk / milk like substance oozes and thorny tree will always be inauspicious for the house owner. Thorny trees always cause misery and torment and fruit bearing trees pave the way for a constant threat of theft. Possibly due to the said reasons our ascetics issued such instructions.

(XI) Tree-Plantation Plan in modern Buildings

10) Trees of banana, jasmine, red-coloured and fragrant flowers, having attractive flowers are considered auspicious, if planted near the boundary wall or entrance gate.

11) According to treatises banyan tree in the east direction, fig tree in the south, pipal in the west and Indian fig tree in the north direction are auspicious. but do not plant any tree, which resembles like golden colour, in the mid-way to the house.

12) Scholars have eulogised and recommended plantation of a holy basil (Tulsi) plant at any place in the house, as this plant has nectar like medicinal properties; hence its utility and sancitity.

Q. Can thorny bushes be planted within the boundary wall of a house?

Ans. No thorny bushes should ever be planted within compound of a house, including all the varieties of cactus, jujube and acacea tree (Babool tree). A tamarind tree is not harmful at all, but should not be planted in east, north-east, north directions, but can be planted in south and west directions. This guideline also applies to all the other big trees which can be planted in south, west directions and largely open spaces.

Q. On which sides of the compound trees should and should not be planted?

Ans. Sturdy trees, like coconut, can be planted from southern sides of south-west direction to south-east and on sides of south-west and north-west directions. But no tree should ever be planted in the north, east and north-east directions. But small flower plants can be planted.

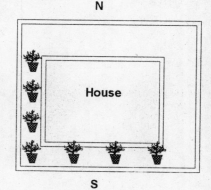

Q. Explain in details about — Chhaya-Vedha (छाया–वेध)?

Ans. It simply means the ill effects caused by any shadow that falls on a built up building. It is of 4 types, Viz.

82

World's longest wall
This picture pertains to China's famous 'Great wall' which is one of the 'seven wonders of the world.' It protects the Chinese from the warriors coming from the northern side. Its length is said to be about 1230 metres..

1) There should not be presence of any hill / mountain on the northern side of a village and its shadow should not fall upon the village at the time of sunrise. If shadow of mountain falls outside the village, it is an auspicious sign.

2) Similarly, shadow of a big tree should not fall on the smaller house. If the big tree is at a farther distance, its shadow would not fall on the house and if the tree falls down, it will not fall upon the house, nor will it cause any harm to the built up house.

3) Shadow of any temple / worship place should not also fall upon any house / It is another type of 'Chhaya Vedha'. As temples always remain flooded with visitors and crowd swells when there are festivals. Crowd is also present in the morning, hence all the temples should have enough wide space outside the vicinity of such temples. As a rule no house should exist upto the space, where shadow of a flag falls. Our ancient scholars must have been guided by such considerations when they formulated the said rules, and these are realistic conclusions also. See figure No. 5, a flag was flying in front of a hotel and shadow of the flag was ominous for the owner of the hotel, as he suffered from some serious ailment. When I ordered removal of the flag, as per Vaastu remedies, treatment started showing favourable results and he regained health.

See figure 6 above. It was a memorial built in the memory of army men.

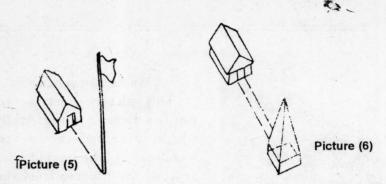

Picture (6)

Picture (5)

Shadow of the memorial fell upon a house and all its occupants died, in due course of time, one-by-one. There should be no pillar, tomb or memorial building in front of a house. Hence it is wiser to avoid such obstructions caused by falling shadows.

4) It should also be ensured that shadow of one's own house should not fall on a well, as this is also an ominous sign.

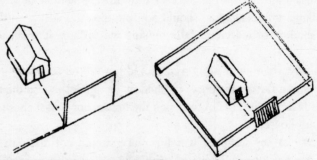

Q. What is meant by 'Drishti Vedha' (दृष्टि–वेध)?

Ans. It is of seven types, viz. (a) If the house owner is not able to see the frontal part of the house, especially where people sit (b) Door of the opposite house is not at a level and it is situated at a lower level. (c) When idol of a deity is not at its appropriate place, and cannot be seen. Idol of deity is installed at a place so that it can be easily seen from a meeting place or gate of the temple. On festival days there is great rush in the temple's compound, hence the devotees should be able to view the idol through main gate (d) If the house gives a horrible look (e) When doors of two houses are opposite each other (f) The doors of two houses are built in such a way that the activities going on in one house, could be viewed from another house (g) When door of one house is faced with double the number of gates.

Above mentioned 'Vedha Doshas' have been formulated, keeping in view social customs and social civilization, hence a house should always be free from the said faults.

Q. What is unplaced by 'Deepalaya Vedha' (दीपालय–वेध)?

Ans. There is a bolt inside an entrance gate. While coming out of the house, there is a hole on the right side of the wall, wherein an earthen lamp (Diya) is kept. As a rule, the hole and bolt ought be at level with each other. If it is not so, it constitutes 'Deepalaya Vedh'.

Q. What is meant by the term 'Koopa-Vedha' (कूप–वेध)?

Ans. If there exists a well or a pit opposite a house or if shadow of the well falls on the house, it is known as 'Koopa-Vedha'.

Q. What the term 'Devasthan Vedha' stands for (देवस्थान–वेध)?

Ans. This type of obstruction emanates from 'Nabhi Vedha', hence refer to 'Nabhi-Vedh' (Vedha-Vaastu Prabhakar)

Q. What is meant by 'Kone-Vedha' (कोण–वेध)?

Ans. When corner of one's own house lies exactly opposite the entrance gate of another house, then 'Kone-Vedha' surfaces, which is also a Vaastu-Fault. Persons, residing in such a house, will not attain the results in comparison to the quantum of efforts put in, that is one has to labour very hard but will gain only numerical benefits. Hence entrance gate should not be impacted by the corner of another house.

(XII) Veethi-Prahar and Veethi-Prasar

Q. What is meant by 'Veethi-Prahar' and 'Veeti-Prasar' terms (वीथि–प्रहार एवं वीथि–प्रसार)?

Ans. The word 'Veethi' means a lane or a path, 'Prahar' means entry into a house or kick/blow. The word 'Prahar' means 'extension or expansion'. Effect and result of 'Prasar' is always negative and that of 'Prasar' is positive. In a way, 'Prahar' is another kind of 'Vedh' which needs to be pondered over, so results of 'Prahar' are bad but that of 'Prasar' are good.

Q. In which directions and paths extensions are auspicious?

Ans. Extensions are considered auspicious in the south portion of south-west direction, western portion of north-west direction, north-portion of north-east direction and eastern portion of north-east direction.

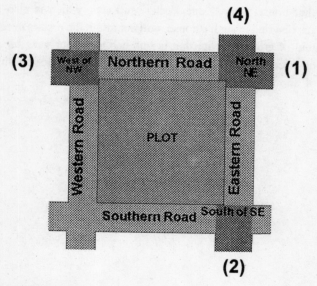

Result of extensions

1. Extension on the northern road / lane of north-east direction imparts authority.

2. Extension on the southern lane / road imparts wealth and prosperity.

3. Extension on the western lane / road imparts the house owner plenty of comforts and prosperity.

4. Extension on the northern road / lane unparts prosperity, wealth and comforts of wife.

Q. What will happen if the road /lane extends beyond the entire area?

Ans. If such type of extensions emerge on the north and east sides, it will be auspicious but on the west and south sides, it will be ominous.

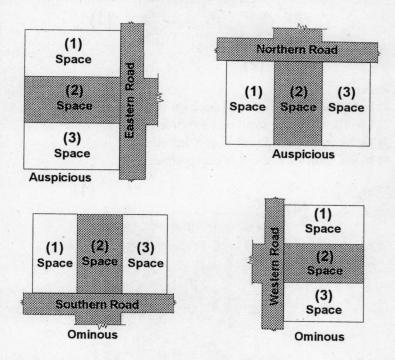

Q. In which of the sides of lanes, extensions are inauspicious?

Which auspicious and inauspicious Veethi-Prahar will follow when extensions ('Veethi Prahar') are connected with north-east, south-east and north-west corners?

Ans. When Veethi-Prahar occurs in the north-east direction, it will be auspicious, but in all else directions, it will be inauspicious, as can be confirmed and ascertained from the following diagram.

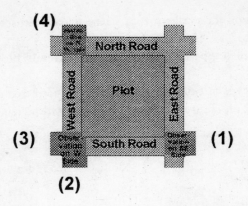

Results :

1) Extension in the north-east direction is highly auspicious.
2) Obstruction in the south-east direction is bad.
3) In the south-west direction, it is inauspicious.
4) In the north-west also it is inauspicious.

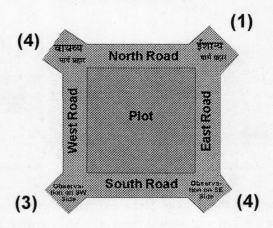

Q. Please explain how 'Veethi Prahar' can be averted?

Ans. If there is violation from the eastern side of south-east direction of a house / plot, then the plot or areas lying opposite, should be disposed off. But if such a 'sold out plot is purchased by another person, he will not get affected by this fault. If it is not possible to dispose of such a vacant plot, build a small room in the corner and also a boundary wall, then sell the same. Now the said suggested change will convert into an auspicious extension and whosoever purchases this plot and builds a house, (he) will roll in wealth. If he consturcts a bunglow, he should also construct a structure over that room. This way an ominous house/plot will turn into an auspicious one. Following diagrams will help to understand what has been explained above. Follow the directions given in the diagrams.

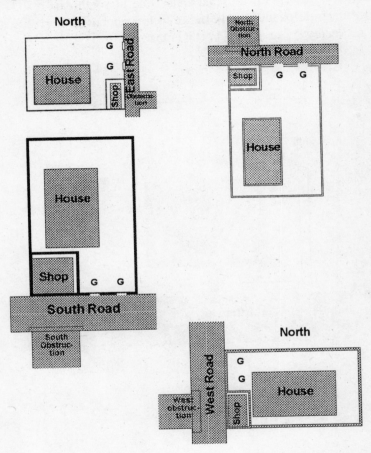

Q. According to some Vaastu experts and scholars, consider extension towards south side of south-east direction as inauspicious. How far is it correct?

Ans. Such statements are delivered by novice and inexperienced persons only. Truly speaking, what is condemned as 'Veethi Prahar' is actually Veethi Prasar. For example, take the case of Shri Venkateshwar Mandir (Temple) which is a Veethi Prasar for the Swami. Tirupati Temple is the richest temple and it is only due to Veethi Prasar. Dovotees throng to this temple from all sides of our country, due to this factor only. Hence it is the greatest Vaastu miracle.

One of my acquaintances has a factory (see the following diamgram). Its extension of path is towards the south side of south-east road, but it is progressing by leaps and bounds. Hence such extentions are not faulty, because they are Veethy Prasar and not Veethi Prahar.

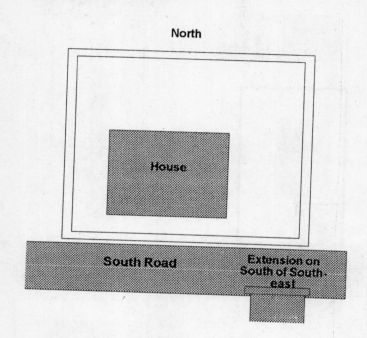

(XIII) Doors, Windows and Ventilators

Q. How many doors and windows should there be in a house?

Ans. There are no fixed indications in this regard. When we enter any house, we can at once read whole history of a house. It hardly matters if there are 13 doors, or whether there are numbers of doors divisible by 2 (like 2, 4, 6, 8, 10, 12, 14, 16, 18), that is in even numbers, or by odd or prime numbers like 1, 3, 5, 7, 9, 11, 13, 15, 17, 19) or if the number ends on zero (like 10, 20 etc.). This concept also applies equality to windows and ventilators. So, number of doors, windows and ventilators is of no consequence.

Q. How the doors should be constructed in a house?

Ans. Doors should not be fixed in such a way that they closely touch the walls. **Hildreth** of a door should be fixed in such a way that a gap of 4", at least should left between the **hildreth** and frame of the door.

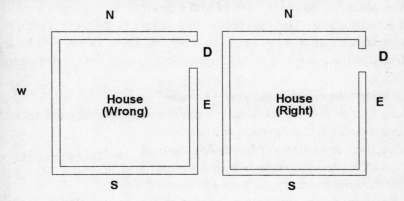

Q. Which of the doors are auspicious in a house and why?

Ans. Eastern door is auspicious. Southern, door on the south-east direction is said to be good for ladies of the house and the householder, the western door ensures welfare, western sided gate on the north-west direction imparts multiple benefit and well-being, northern gate yields progress, northern gate on the north-east direction brings in fortune and eastern gate on this direction enhances all-round fame.

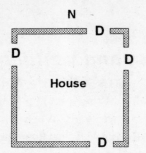

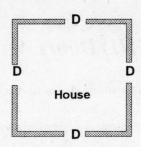

Q. What is meant by 'Main gate'?

Ans. Main gate is never affixed to the boundary wall. A main gate is the main entrance gate which lies after the boundary wall. It is also called 'Singha Dwaar'. It is comparatively bigger, larger more strong and more beautiful than all other gates in the house. If main gate in a house is in perfect order, then entire house will be in order.

Q. What are the necessary points and considerations in respect of the main gate?

Ans. Main gate should be studded with auspicious emblems like, swastik emblem, bells, onkar, Ganpati's idol/picture, lamp etc. Its height should be one foot higher than average height of a person. There should also be no 'Vedh' and, if there is any, it should be dispelled, by corrective and remedial methods.

Q. Which doors are considered Ominous?

Ans. Eastern door on south-east direction can inflame fire and attracts thieves and causes illness. Southern gate on the south-west direction causes illness to the female inmates of the house and western gate on the same direction causes death of the male members, northern gate on north-west direction causes restivity impatience to the inmates of the house. Due to the aforesaid factors, such type of doors are not considered auspicious.

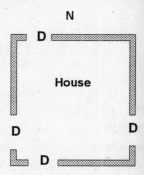

Arched Gateway

If you have already built your house doors have also affixed, but Door-Fault (Dwaar Dosha) is causing problems, you need not worry. To dispel this fault use a 'Vaastu-dosha Nashak Toran' which will offset the damaging effects and yield auspicious results for you.

(XIV) Entry and Exit Points

Q. Which of the entries are considered auspicious for entry and exit in a house?

Ans. Following types of doors are considered good for entry and exit in a house.

1. From west to south, from south of south-east direction to north side of north-east direction.
2. From south to north, from western side of north-west direction to eastern side of norht-east direction.
3. From the western to north side of north-east direction and to east side.
4. From east side of north-east direction to northern side of and west.
5. From north of north-east direction to south and from east of north-east direction. These positions have been explained through following diagrams.

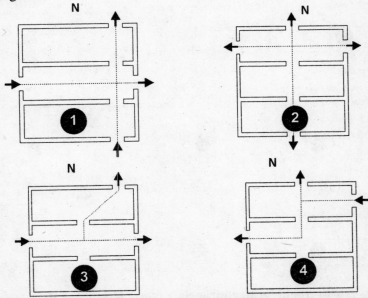

Q. Which of the entry points are not considered auspicious to make an entry into a house?

Ans. Following entry point are not considered auspicious for movements in a house.

1. From south of south-east direction to north and east sides of north-east

direction.

2. From western side of south-west direction to east and north sides of north-east direction.

3. From west of north-west direction to south and east direction of south-east direction.

4. From west to east of south-east direction and south side of south-east direction.

5. From south and east to north side of north-west direction.

6. From south to west and east of south-west direction.

7. From east and south of south-east direction to the north side.

8. From east to west of south-west direction, from south side of south-west direction and north to south of south-west direction, western side of south-west direction.

9. West to south, while passing through the south-east direction.

10. From south to west of north-west direction. The said points have been more clearly explained through the following diagrams.

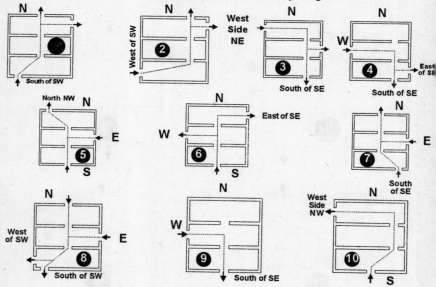

Q. Which would be an appropriate place, if only one door is desired to be affixed in a house?

Ans. If only one door is desired to be installed in a house, the same should be installed in the eastern or northern side of north-east direction. This is how even a single door will cause excellent results and gains. No other door should be affixed in those houses (which have already main gate) in the west and south sides. If the house owner builds a house for personal, then he should never opt for such houses. There will, however, be no Vaastu fault involved if only a single door is built in the south-west and north-east rooms.

Q. Where and how should two doors be affixed?

Ans. Doors can be affixed like this — East or west or north or south or east to north.

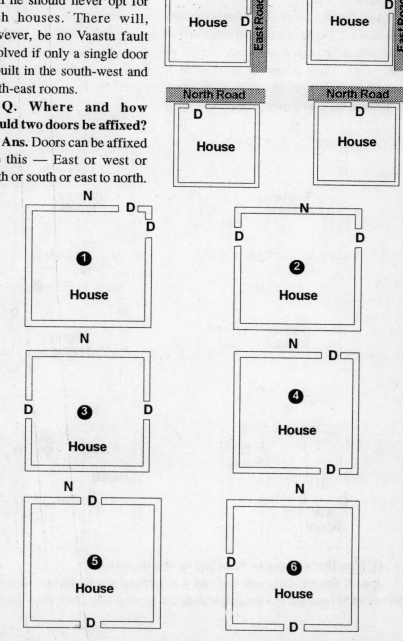

But no door should be affixed towards west and south directions.

Q. If three doors are required to be affixed, on which directions should the same be built?

Ans. Gates / doors should not be built on any other direction, without an eastern door. Doors can be built on all directions, except the southern direction. Similarly doors can also be built on all directions, but only when northern gate exists. Three doors can be built in any interior room, but three doors should not be built in the south-west direction. Straight doors can be affixed in the internal curvatured walls.

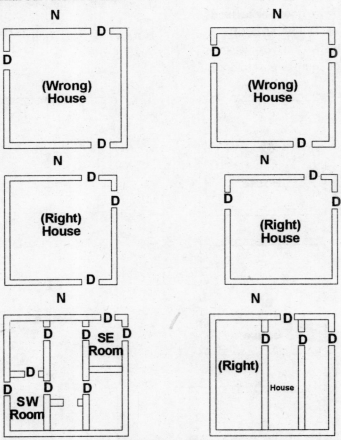

Q. Can three doors be installed in one direction

Ans. If there is only one hall and it is without any partitions, then three doors can be installed in a straight line, as can be seen in the following diagram.

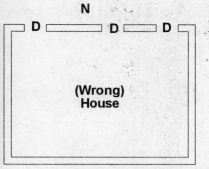

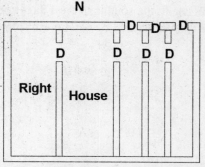

Q. **Which specific rules should be followed when four doors are to be installed?**

Ans. If the house has been built according to the directional norms, then four doors can be installed on all the four sides, but doors can not be installed in south-west room. However, four doors can be installed in a north-east room.

Q. **What should be the directional situations of windows in a house?**

Ans. Doors, windows and almirahs should be opposite to each other. If there are doors on all sides of a house, these should be kept on a higher or medium height. It is possible only when construction of a house conforms to Vaastu directions.

Q. **Can windows be affixed in the wall, outside or inside of a wall or else in the mid part?**

Ans. Windows are installed for protection of a house; hence it is better if those are installed within the wall and in the centre part.

Q. **Should grills and arches also be deemed as doors?**

Ans. Some persons deem grills and arches as doors, as long as they continue to touch and adhere to the roof.

Q. **Which of the doors in a house are not deemed as doors?**

Ans. Doors of kitchen, bathroom and small rooms will not be deemed as doors, until they do not touch the roof. Similarly, rods or partitions will not also be deemed as doors which are used to for wind, light and protection of a house.

Q. **Where should the doors be built in a house whose north, east, south or west portion touches another house?**

Ans. When a house touches another house in the north and east sides, its construction will not be good, due to coverage of north and east sides. There is nothing bad and wrong if some area is left vacant in the north and east directions and then construction of house is initiated. If the house touches a house in the south and west direction, then it will be in order to install a door / gate in the east or / and north side of north-east direction.

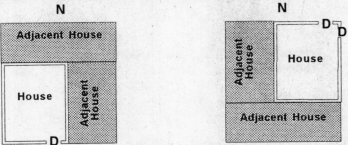

Q. If a house is touched by houses on its both the sides, then where the door should be installed?

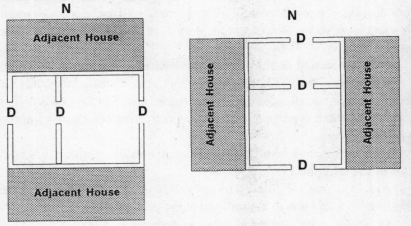

Ans. See the above diagrame.

Remarks : In the above position, three doors can be installed in the middle part of the house from north to south and east to west.

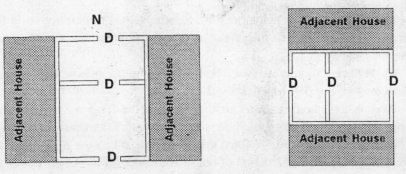

Three doors can be installed from the north side of north-east direction to the south side of south-east direction.

Three doors can be installed from the east side of north-east direction to west side of the north-west direction.

Specific guidelines about shops only

Q. Where should be seat of a shopkeeper in an east-facing shop?

Ans. Construct a shopping floor, from west to east and south to north, which should be away from eastern wall of south-east direction, but should touch the southern wall of south-east direction. When it has been done, as suggested above the shopkeeper should sit facing the north side and keep his cash box to his left side.

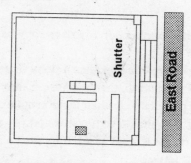

Q. Can one sit in the the same seat, while facing the eastern side?

Ans. Yes, one can sit in that direction, facing east, but he should keep the cash-box or almirah to his left side.

Q. Can a person construct a platform and then sit thereon?

Ans. Sitting on a built up platform is prohibited. But if it is not convenient to sit on the floor, a chair and a table can be placed for sitting. But never sit on north and west corners of north-west direction. A sitting platform should be slightly higher than the plinth level of floor.

Q. If the main gate of a shop is south-facing, where should the shop-owner sit?

Ans. Floor should be slopy from south to east and west to east directions, then a platform should be raised and the shop-owner should place his chair or table thereon and then sit or else sit on the raised platform, while his face should be towards the east direction. Cash box should be placed on his right side. The owner should not carry on any business activity, by sitting on the south-east, north-west and north-east directions, if main gate of his shop is south-facing.

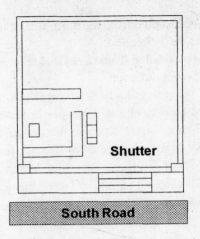

Shutter

South Road

**Q. Where should the shopkeeper (owner) sit when his shop's ga[r]
faces western direction?**

Ans. If door of a shop is west-facing, then a slopy flooring should be bu[i]
from west to east and south to north, then a platform should be raised whe[re]
the shopkeeper should or place table & chair thereon or he can sit on the rais[ed]
platform also but then his face should be towards north — in this situation t[he]
cash box should be kept on the left side. But, if he sits facing east side, cas[h]
box should be kept on his left side.

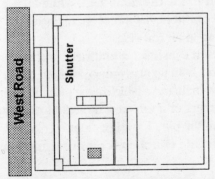

West Road

Shutter

**Q. Where should the shop-owner be seated if his shops door falls [on]
the northern side?**

Ans. If the door of a shop is north-facing, then a slopy flooring should [be]
made from south to west and from west to east but away (nor touching) [the]
northern wall of north-west direction, though the platform should adhere to[u]
the western wall or place a table and chair thereon — the shop-owner sho[uld]
sit in the chair and conduct his business activity and keep the cash-box on [...]

100

eft side. But, if he prefers to sit facing the northern direction, he should keep
he cash box on his right side.

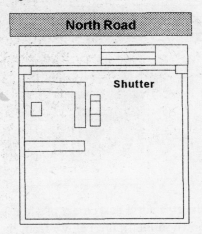

Q. Can a trading shopkeeper can himself conduct the business dealings
if he builds a shop in the north-east, south-east and north-west corner of
his house?

Ans. As is shown in the following figure, a shopkeeper can build a shop in
the south-east corner of his house and conduct his business or he can rent out
his shop to another person to conduct business.

Other Options : Or alternatively, the shopkeeper can conduct his business
activities by building a shop in the south-west direction of his house or give
his shop on rental basis to someone else to conduct business activities.

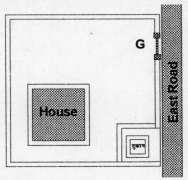

He can also build a shop in the north-west corner of his house where he
himself can trade or else lease his shop on rental basis to someone else. In the
following figures, shutters have also been shown in the house and shop and

also entry gates on all the four sides.

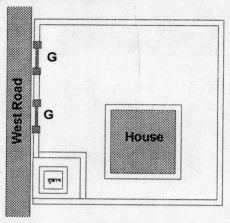

When a shop is built in the north-east corner of a house, then an entry gate should be made (as shown in the figure below) from the house (inside the shop to effect entry), and the owner should conduct his business, but never lease the shop to any other person. But, it is a fact, which very few people know, that a shop should not be built to the north-east direction of the house.

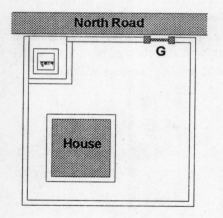

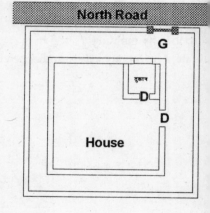

(XV)
Stairs, shutters and entrance in a shop

Q. Which is an ideal place for building stairs in an east-facing shop?

Ans. Stairs should be constructed on the northern side of north-east direction or wide stairs can be built in the entire length of the shop. If it is not possible, then a platform should be raised on the south-east side of the house, whereafter stairs can be constructed in the north-east direction. In such cases stairs are required to be constructed in the northern side of north-east direction.

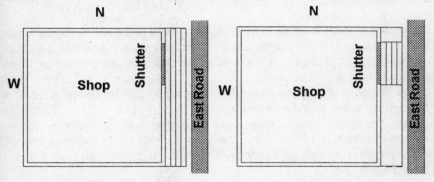

Q. Where should the stairs be constructed in a shop whose main-gate is west-facing?

Ans. Stairs should be constructed in the north-west side. Or a platform should be raised on the south-west side, in the centre portion of the shop, and stairs built on the remaining part. If it is possible, semi-circular (half moon shaped) may also be built.

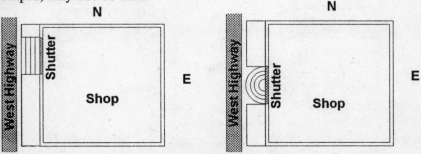

103

Q. Which is the suitable place to construct stairs in a shop whose main-gate is north-facing?

Ans. See the following figures and related guidelines.

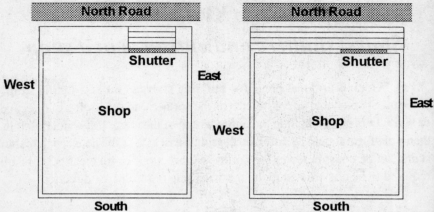

In such a situation stairs are required to be built in the north-east direction or else build stairs from north-west to north-east direction. If possible, construct a platform in the mid-part of north-west direction and then construct stairs towards the north-east direction.

Q. Which is an appropriate site where stairs can be constructed in a shop whose main door faces south side?

Ans. In such a type of shop stairs can be built in the southern side of south-east direction, or else stairs can also be built along southern side of south-east and south-west directions. If possible, you can build even semi — circular stairs also.

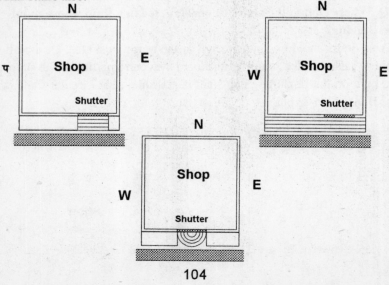

Q. Which shutter should be kept opened in a shop whose main gate is west-facing?

Ans. In such a type of shop, north-western shutters can be kept opened and south-western shutter kept closed (shut) or else both should be kept opened.

But, always keep in mind, never to open the south-west shutter and shut with the north-west shutter, as it will create problems if north-west shutter is used to close a shutter.

Q. Which shutter should be kept closed in a shop whose main gate faces northern side?

Ans. North-eastern shutter should be kept opened and the north-west shutter kept shut, or else both shutters can be kept opened. But

never open with the north-west shutter and close with the north-east shutter. If north-sided shutter, something should be placed in the northern shutter of north-eastern direction.

Q. Which is an ideal place to keep heavy machinery in a factory premises?

Ans. Heavy machinery should be kept or installed in the north-west direction of a factory. But some machines to be kept only upto the flooring level, hence a pit should be dug up in the east and north sides and then machines installed therein.

Q. Which is the preferred site for a godown.

Ans. Most suitable site for a godown is the south-west direction and for the boiler, it is the south-east direction.

Q. Which site is most suited for the office of the factory owner?

Ans. If a factory has doors in the east and west directions, then factory owner's office should be in the southern direction, because godowns are constructed in the northern direction. But, if gate is situated on the north and south sides and godown is situated on the east and west, then factory owner's seat or office will have to be built in the western direction.

Q. Where balance / scale should be kept in the shop?

Ans. It should be kept on a platform or floor, along the side of western and southern walls.

Q. Which is an ideal place for keeping a showcase?

Ans. Showcase, almirah, stand etc. are heavy objects, hence those can be kept on any side but never on the north-east side.

Q. Where should the shop-owner live in a shop?

Ans. A trader should live in a room that is situated in the south-west direction and he should face north or east directions while sitting.

Q. On which direction should the door of shop-owner's room be?

Ans. The owner's room should have its door in the east, north or east or north sides of north-east direction but not in the south-east, south-west and north-west directions.

Q. If a shop has two shutters — which one should be kept, closed or which one kept opened?

Ans. Eastern shutter, on the north direction, should be kept opened and south-east shutter should be kept closed, or else both the shutters can be kept opened. But never open the south-eastern shutter by closing the north-eastern shutter. If, at all, it is opened it should not move from the same portion and to close the route, put up a partition or use a bench in the transverse form.

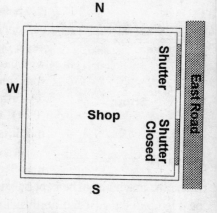

Q. Which portion of the shutter should be shut, in a shop which has a south-facing gate?

Ans. Open the shutter of the south-east direction and close the south-west shutter. But never close the south-east shutter, if you have already opened the south-eastern shutter. If it becomes necessery to open it, place some hurdle in its way.

106

(XVI)
Guidelines about Factories and Industries

Boiler, furnace etc. should always be kept in the south-east corner only in a factory, industry or plot of land. But it should never be in the north-east corner, because air and fire are inherent and natural enemies. Since seat of Varun (lord of water) is in the north-east direction and if a boiler is kept on this side, it is liable to land a factory in troubles. To ensure success and prosperity of a unit, all the gadgets which have direct connection with fire or heat, (like generator, transformer, electric supply, heavy machinery, boiler, heater etc., should always be kept in the south-east direction. Boiler etc. should also not be kept in the central position or south-west side of a factory.

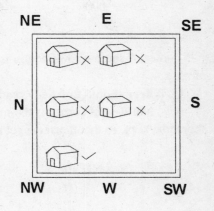

Q. Which is the most suitable place in a factory area, where labour quarters should be built.

Ans. Quarters for labour should always be built in the north-west corner of a factory, but no labour quarter should be built in the east, north or north-east directions, as neither the workers nor the officers will comply with orders of the industrialist and flout his command.

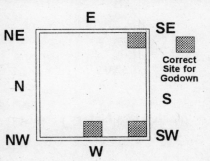

Q. Where should a godown be located in a factory?

Ans. SW : Godown in a factory should be located in **SW** direction and all the useless, redundant things should also be kept in the south-west direction.

S : If there exists no suitable south,

W : west corner in a factory, then godown can be provided for in the western or southern directions.

Effective Result : Stored goods will be quickly sold off if kept in godowns, built in south-west, south or western directions.

Q. Which is an ideal site to install a boiler in a factory?

Ans. Place of boiler in a factory.

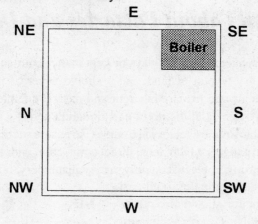

Corner of south-east direction is the most ideal place for a boiler in any factory.

Q. Where should finished / ready goods be kept in a factory premises?

Ans. North-west corner is the most suitable place where finished goods should be kept, so that the same get quickly disposed of.

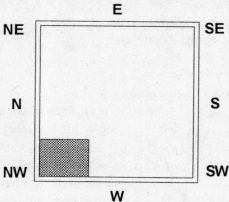

Q. Which type of trees should not be planted in a factory premises?

Ans. Prohibited Plantation of trees.

खजूरी दाड़िमी रम्भा कर्कन्धू बीज पूरिका।
उत्पद्यन्ते गृहे यत्र तस्मिन कृत्तति मूलतः॥

Which means that a house will remain feudridden and ultimately will be doomed if there is self-growth of palm, pomegranate, jujube and lemon (of Bijaura quality) trees or plants —this principle applies equally to the factories also.

Trees which are inauspicious and endanger life and cause pain.

A tree bearing yellow fragrant flowers, tree with large sized jasmine flowers, fragrant flower pandanus, Paakar, shallow and termite-ridden fig tree, milk-oozing and throny plants and trees should not be grown or allowed to grow in an outside vicinity of building / factory. All such trees and plants are inauspicious, as they cause agony, tormentation and illness to the owner of house.

(XVII) VERANDAHS

Q. Which type of Verandah should be built in a house?

Ans. Western side should be higher than the eastern side of a verandah, southern side should be higher than the northern side of verandah. Eastern side of a verandah should be wider than the western side and northern side should be higher than the southern side, and width should be slightly wider.

Q. Which types of verandah are considered good or bad in a house?

Ans. Both types of good and bad verandahs have been known by means of the following diagrams.

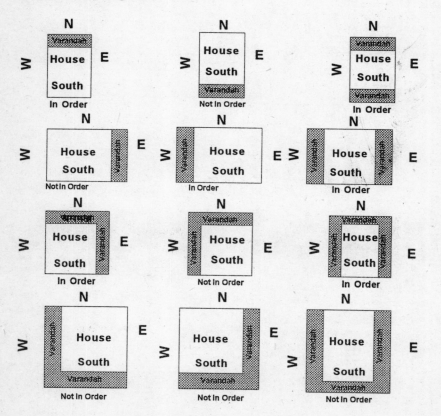

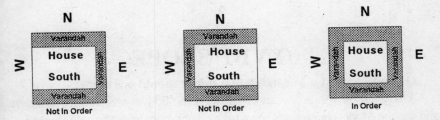

| Not In Order | Not In Order | In Order |

Q. What should be the pattern of slope in the Verandah of a house?

Ans. These types of verandahs should have higher plinth (height) in the west and south than east and north verandahs or can be also at identical plinth. But width of east and north verandahs should be more as compared to the width of west and south verandahs.

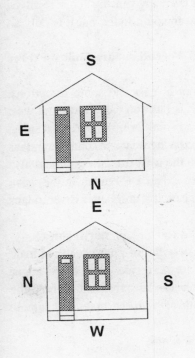

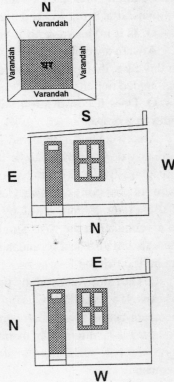

111

(XVIII) SLOPE

Q. How slope of a Verandah in a house should me made?

Ans. Sloping verandah can be made in the houses which have southern and western doors (main gates) or where height of the main house is higher — in the later case, plinth of the sloping verandah should be slightly raised. But on the west and south sides of the house, sloping verandahs should not be compressed also but should be at lesser height than the height of the house.

Q. What are the guidelines for making verandahs in such houses whose main gates are east and north facing?

Ans. It is better to keep plinth level low.

Q. Is it a Vaastu-fault if verandahs are made all around the house?

Ans. In my opinion there is no harm, nor even any Vaastu-fault is involved in this case, though such a belief is nurtured in south India, but it is only an unfounded notion.

Q. Does it constitute a vaastu-fault if Verandahs are built on three sides in a house?

Ans. No fault is involved if built on north, east and south directions. Similarly no fault will also be if a verandah is built on east, north and west directions. But, if slope is kept on the east and south or north and west sides, there is a possibility of losses. Generally, slope on the west and south verandahs is also a fault. If there is a slopy verandah on the west side, there should also be a verandah in the east. Similarly, if there exists a verandah in the west, there should also be a verandah in the north. But, it is still better if verandahs are built on all the four sides.

Q. Can slopy verandahs be also built in the east or north sides?

Ans. If a verandah exists only in the east, it will safe-guard health of male members but, if a verandah is built on the northern side only, it will augur well for the health of lady members. But, if verandahs are built on both the north and east sides, it will safeguard health of both the male and famale members.

'Back Yard' of a house

Q. What is meant by 'Back-Side'?

Ans. Back yard, part or portion of the house is known as 'Back Side'. A portion of the house which has been segregated from the house, or a portion away from the house or has been segregated from another house, is also nomencleted by these terms.

Q. Which types of backyard are considered good and auspicious?

Ans. The house in which we reside, will prove good if there is double the open space vacant in the east and north sides of north-east direction. That is, if a boundary is drawn on the north and east sides, the north-east direction should look actually extended. So, it is an auspicious sign; if the backyards exist in the backyard of the house in the east and north ends of north-east direction. If you will study the following diagrams, you can confirm what has been mentioned above.

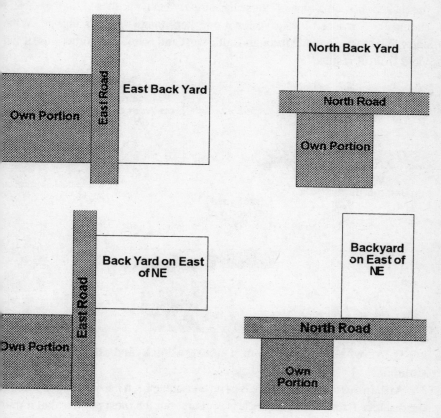

Q. Which types of backyards are inauspicious?

Ans. If in east side of south-east direction or north side of north-west direction, there exist many backyards and when a line is drawn (with reference to our own house) then it will be inauspicious when the north-east side reduces (that is, it does not extend).

113

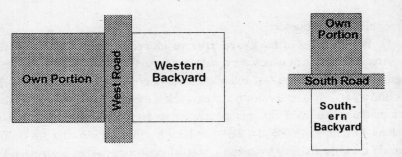

If a backyard exists in the south-west direction of a house, it should not be purchased. If such a type of house has already been purchased, in that case, it should be converted into a godown and kept under owner's charge. When entry and exist are made through south-west and south-east directions, it will yield fruitful results.

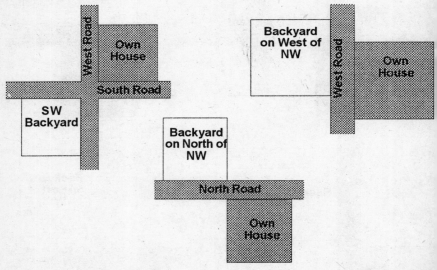

Q. At what distance from a house a backyard should be kept or situated?

Ans. In this context distance is of no consequence, it hardly matters whether the distance (from the house) is less or more, but the most point is that it must be frequently visited.

Q. On which directions should backyards exist?

Ans. In this regard following conditions should determine the exact position — the backyard should extend from north-east direction, should be weighty or heavy in the south-west direction and light and lowly in the north-east direction.

(XIX) BALCONY

Q. Which type of balcony is ideal and how should it be built?

Ans. Width of a southern balcony should be more than the western balcony, and eastern balcony should be more than the western balcony. If this situation can be ensured then only it will Constitute correct vaastu.

Q. How should doors be erected within the rooms which have balconies?

Ans. A room should be built in the corner of an eastern verandah and then northern gate should be erected on a higher plinth, but do not construct any room in the north-east. Construct a room in the southern corner of north-west verandah, and then affix, on higher plinth, a door on eastern side. No room should be built in the south-east direction and no room should also be built in the north-west direction. Construct a room in the western corner of the Verandah (on the south-west direction) and then affix a door, on higher plinth, towards the north side. On the north side of north-west verandah construct a room and instal a door, on higher plinths, in the east. It is not auspicious to construct a room in the north-east direction.

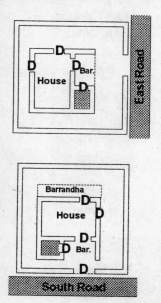

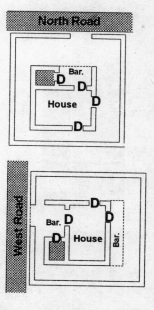

Q. Which are the conditions under which a pruned (cut) balcony is considered bad or good?

Ans. Balcony should not be constructed in the north, east sides and north

115

east direction. At times, construction of a balcony is not considered bad in the south side of south-east, south side of south-west, west side of south-west, western side of north-west, even if the balcony is pruned on these sides. See the following diagrams.

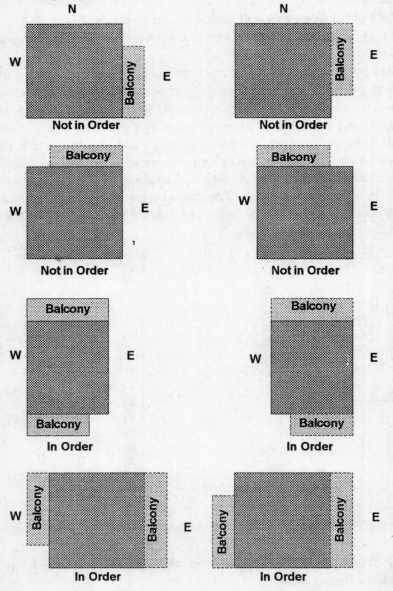

(XX) Detailed description about stairs

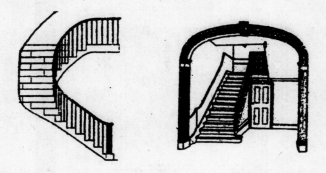

Q. Stairs to the terrace should be from within the house or outside?

Ans. Stairs should be built within the house from east to west or north to south, but never build stairs from west to east or from south to north to reach the terrac.

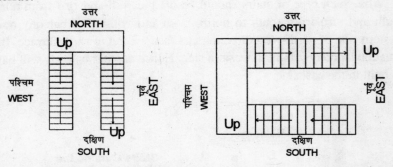

Q. How should stairs be built in the eastern side of south-east direction in a house?

Ans. Stairs should be away from north-east to west or north to south, but never build stairs from west to east or from south to north to reach the terrace.

Q. How should stairs be built in the eastern side of south-east direction in a house?

Ans. Stairs should be away from north-east boundary wall. Build stairs from north to south so that one has to ascend the stairs by taking a turn from south to north. Such stairs should pass through the balcony made in the east corner of north-east direction to ascend the stairs. No pillars should be built under the stairs but it will be better if beams are built instead of pillars.

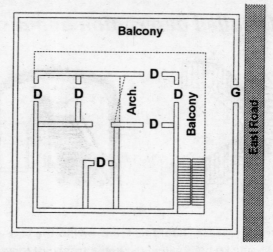

Q. How should stairs be constructed in the western side of south-west direction?

Ans. Such type of stairs should be off the wall and rise from north to south and turn from south to north, from and within the balcony built in western side of north-west direction and then ascend towards terrace. In this situation balcony is built in western side. Hence another balcony will have to be built in the east side.

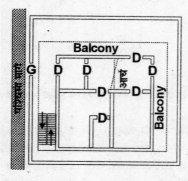

Stairs Outside the Western Main Gate

Q. How stairs should be constructed on the northern side of north-west direction?

Ans. This type of stairs should not touch the northern boundary wall, but should ascend from east to west, then should take a turn from west to east and pass through the northern side of north-east direction of the already built balcony and then ascend to reach the top.

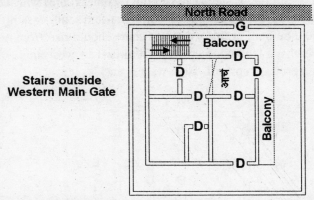

Stairs outside Western Main Gate

Q. How should stairs be built in the southern side of south-west direction?

Ans. This type of stairs will ascend from east to west, then take a turn (curve) from west to east in the upward form in the southern side of south-east direction and pass through the balcony and then reach the top. A balcony has already been built in the southern side, so it is necessary to build another balcony in the north. Raise a beam, but not a pillar underneath the stairs.

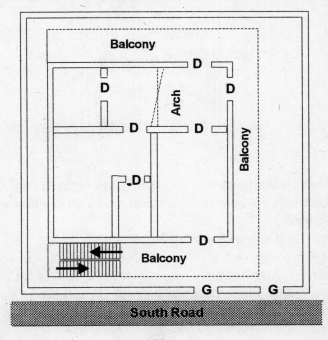

119

Q. How circuitous or meandering stairs be built within the house?

Ans. Spiral or Circuitous stairs can be built by other rooms which do not form part of north side rooms of north-east direction and south-east direction. Such stairs should be built in this way: first stairs should rise from north to south, then ascend for landing, then turn from east to west, then rise for landing, and then proceed upwards from west to east.

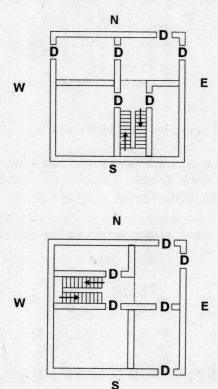

Above mentioned guidelines are required to be followed while constructing stairs in the outside portion of the house in south-east, south-west and north-west directions.

Q. How will you spell out landing of stairs?

Ans. While constructing stairs in the west and south or in north-west or south-east directions, which are proximate touching to the outer wall, landing should be towards the western and southern sides. It hardly matters if the landing extends beyond the alignment (straightness) of the house.

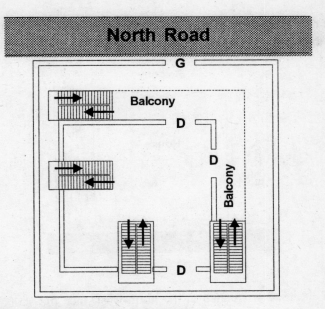

Q. How should stairs be constructed?

Ans. Round / circuitous stairs can be constructed in any house which has a main gate. This type of stairs can be built in the southern side of south-east direction or western side of north-west direction, but a balcony must be built in each of the eastern and northern sides of the house.

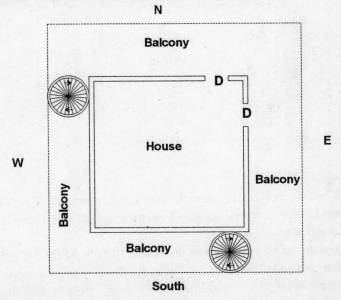

i) If road exists in the south-west direction, then the stairs will have to be built in the south-east, which will extend from south-east to north-west.

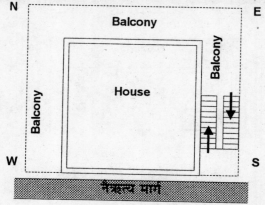

ii) If the road is situated in the north-west, then the stairs should be constructed in the western part which should elevate in the north-east from south-west.

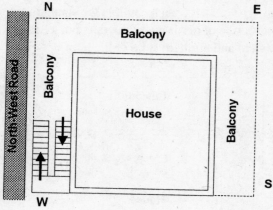

iii) When the road is situated in the north-east, stairs should be built in the southern side of it or western side of north-west and stairs should elevate towards south-west direction.

If stairs are to be built with in the house, then build the stairs in south, west, south-east and north-west, but the stairs should elevate from south-east towards south-west. If stairs are built in the south-west, it will constitute a

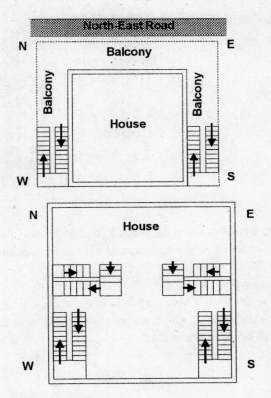

vaastu-fault occurrence of a pit.

Q. Which method should be adopted to construct L-Shaped stairs outside the house?

Ans. Stairs outside the house, which has main doors in the north and west, should elevate from north towards west, then should elevate on a high western site so as to reach the terrace. If the house has eastern and western main gates, then first of all elevate in the east from north to south, then turn to raised elevation on the southern side of south-east direction and then reach the terrace.

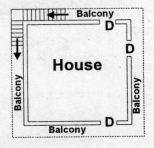
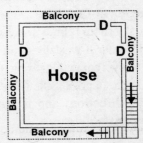

Q. How to build stairs in directionless houses?

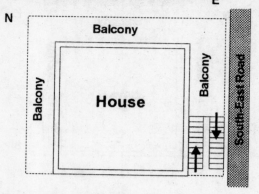

Ans. When a road exists in the south-eastern direction, then stairs should be built in the southern side which should extend from north-east to south-west.

Another example

In the above situation if stairs are built in the north-eastern side, this side will get pruned and tapered which will not only augur well for the residents but this side will become heavy also.

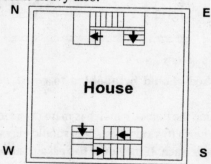

Q. Can a room be constructed under the stairs of the houses, in the north side of north-west direction, whose main gates are north-facing?

Ans. If a room is built under such stairs, then north side of north-west direction will extend. So, in order to overcome this problem, a wall should be built in the opposite side (that is north side of north-east direction) and it should touch the northern part.

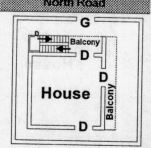

124

Q. Can a bathroom be constructed underneath the landing of stairs in the houses which have main gates is in the east?

Ans. If a bathroom is built under the stairs which elevate from north to west, then north-west side will get extended which is not an auspicious sign. If, at all it is necessary to build a bathroom under the aforesaid situation, then an adjacent wall in the eastern side of north-east direction should be built and in this situation it is necessary to leave more area vacant from west to east.

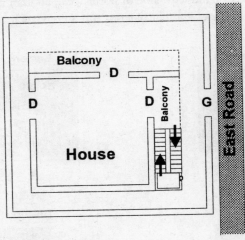

Q. Is it advisable to construct rooms under the stairs of such houses (built in the western side of south-west direction), whose main doors are west facing?

Ans. Such type of rooms should not be built, as height of these rooms will be lower than the height of others rooms in the house.

Q. If main gate of a house is facing south, can a room be built underneath the stairs of such a house?

Ans. No, it is not advisable, as it is prohibited to build any room when the above mentioned conditions exist.

Q. Which type of doors are suitable for the windows of rooms built under the stairs?

Ans. If doors in the rooms, built under the stairs landings, are built on a higher plinth, then it is faultless.

Q. When no vacant space is available outside the house, then can cut-stairs be made in the south-east and north-west directions?

Ans. Such a doubt must have surfaced while alighting from stairs from the terrace in the eastern side of south-east. This is not suited to the persons

125

who go up the terrace. In such a situation if there is no vacant space, then stairs should be built on (1) western side of north west (2) eastern side of south-east (3) northern side of north-west and (4) southern side of south-west. (as already detailed heretofore).

To enter the terrace through the stairs from southern side of south-east, a balcony should be built in the north. If it is not done, northern side will be camouflaged, because a balcony already exists in the south. Similarly, if you enter the terrace from the west side of north-west, another balcony should be built in the east, because another balcony already exists in the west.

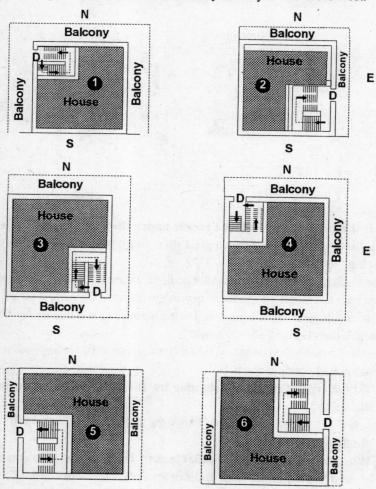

(XXI) Vaastu guidelines in respect of Bed-rooms

Q. Has the Bedroom any importance in Vaastu?

Ans. It is not simply an important aspect in Vaastu, but it is extremly prominent and significant in one's life. Day and night are earmarked natural phenomena. Sleep is an important part of relaxation and every person has his own method in this respect. For instance a dolphin closes her eyes in the flowing water and sleeps in the water, a bat hangs down a tree and sleeps. A hen sleeps while hatching its eggs, little kids fold their feet and sleep in a shrunk form. Whatever be the type of a living being, nature's five-element power compels everyone to sleep. So, a bedroom is like a sleeping temple for the human beings. Actually, bedroom is the heart of a house and it is the only venue in the house where major part of life is spent.

Q. Which is the ideal place to place a bed?

Ans. Sleeping bed should be placed in the south-west direction. The bed should be placed in such a way in the room (bedroom) that reasonable space is left vacant in the east and north direction.

Q.Why should people build a bedroom in the south-west direction and how should it be done?

Ans. Of all the eight directions, south-west is the most benevolent one and that's the reason as to why most people prefer to sleep in south-west direction. Most of the people prefer cold temperature in the bedroom, but it has been proved scientifically that temperature of a bedroom should at least be 60^0 F, as too much cold is detrimental to health.

Q. Could you specify rooms in which each person can sleep?

Ans. Why not. Study the following diagrams and you will yourself realise suitability of room for every dweller in a house.

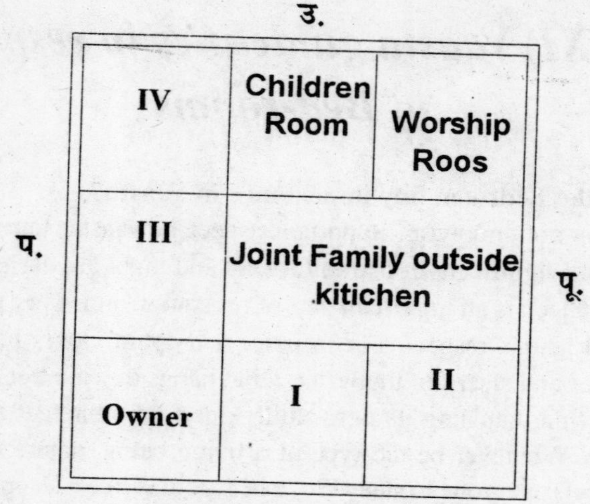

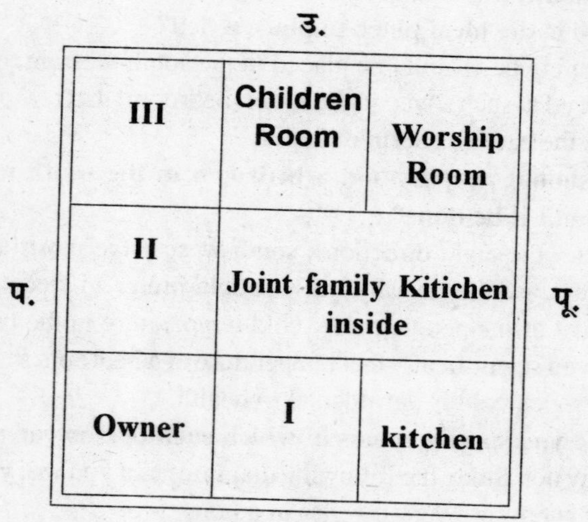

उ.

IV	Children Room	Worship Roos
III	Joint Family outside kitichen	
Owner	I	II

प.　　　　　　　　　　　　　　पू:

उ.

III	Children Room	Worship Room
II	Joint family Kitichen inside	
Owner	I	kitchen

प.　　　　　　　　　　　　　　पू:

Q. On which directions can the head be kept?

Ans. As a general rule, head should be kept towards the southern direction. If it is not feasible, then head can be kept towards the east direction. But keeping head towards the west is prohibited. But, in any case, do not keep your pillow towards the northern direction.

128

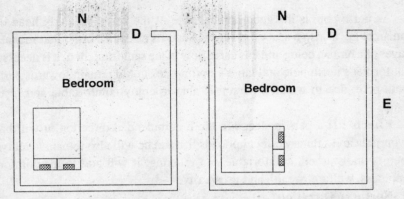

Q. Why head should not be kept in the northern direction?

Ans. If head is kept towards the northern direction, it can cause various ailments and this statement has been repeated by way of many sayings and proverbs. There is a famous proverb which means that vomiting will surely ensue, if one sleeps by keeping the head in the northern direction. I have already explained the relevant detail in this regard, in September 1968 issue of 'Vaishya Prabodhini'.

Q. What are the merits and demerits attached to the fact of sleeping in various directions. Explain also the religious and scientific aspects, reasons and causes also?

Ans. Yes, there are both the scientific and religious considerations and backed by authenticated conclusions, proofs and causes which are detailed hereunder.

Southern Direction

It has been said that : Those, who aspire and wish to enjoy excellent health and long span of life, should always keep their heads (pillows) in the southern direction and feet towards north direction.

Religious reason

Yama, the lord of death, is the lord of southern direction, hence if a person keeps his feet towards this direction, seems as if he is proceeding to embrace death hence, it has been advised to keep head towards south, but not your feet.

Scientific reasons

It has been proved scientifically human body is impacted by magnetic waves, and human body also repels these waves — that it is a recipient and repeller of magnetic waves which create attraction and repulsion in the atmosphere.

As north pole is the geographical pole of the earth, similarly head of a human being is also a seat of north pole and its effect. In order that magnetic waves of a human being and this earth flow in the same direction, it is necessary that former's north pole and latter's north pole should remain towards earth's south pole, due to which a person is able to enjoy comfortable and restful sleep.

Effects : If a person sleeps in the recommended direction, it will have favourable and salutary effect upon his life and he will also remain healthy. If sleep is undisturbed, comfortable and relaxing, it will add to his comforts, happiness, welfare, wealth and prosperity.

Northern Direction

Effect : If a person sleeps while keeping his head towards the northern direction, he can never enjoy a sound sleep. Such persons pass restive nights, continue to turn from one side of the bed to another, change sides quite often. When they get up in the morning they will be tense, restive and have pain in the body. If they sleep in the northern side they will see unreal dreams and seem to be embroiled in unproductive hurdles, their children suffer from many problems. There is always loss of wealth and death-like tormentation by sleeping in the north direction.

Religious reasons — Kuber is the lord and deity of wealth. So, if a person keeps his feet towards north, it will give the impression as if he is proceeding to seek the blessings of Kuber for being blessed with more wealth. Hence, always keep feet towards north and head towards south, but in the reverse position, a person will march towards death and also be deprived of wealth.

Scientific reasons

If a person keeps his head in the north direction, while sleeping, magnetic waves will be adversely affected, distorted and toxified, due to which the person will not enjoy a sound sleep.

Western Direction

Effects : If a person keeps his head towards western direction, he will suffer from various ailments and will be under control of death, in addtition to suffering from worries and anxieties of variable types.

Eastern Direction

By Keeping the head towards the eastern direction, while sleeping, his conscience, soul, spiritual thought will be adversely impacted.

Conclusions

Due to the reasons, cited above, a person should keep his head towards

130

eastern or southern direction, but should not keep his head towards northern and western directions. But, when a person is travelling he can keep his head towards western direction, while sleeping.

Q. Which is an appropriate place for building the Master-Bedroom?

Ans. Bedroom of the house owner is called the Master Bedroom which should be built in the south-west corner of the house.

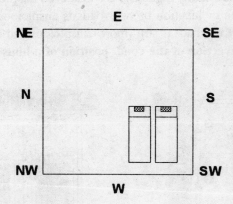

(XXII) HIGHWAY AND ROADS

Q. Junction of how many highways is considered auspicious and good?

Ans. Intersection or junction of two roads is auspicious and good, but junction of three or four roads is still (more) auspicious and better.

Q. On which direction of the road, position of a house is considered auspicioius?

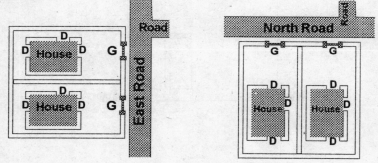

Ans. If the road is situated in the north or east sides of the house, it will straightaway lead to north-east direction or north or east. See the preceding diagrams.

Q. In which sides of the house roads are not considered good, when one leaves one's house?

Ans. When we have already set out and left our house, then the road that leads us to eastern side of south-east direction or east or south, it is not considered to be a good and auspicious road.

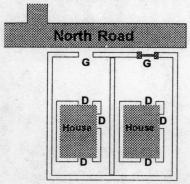

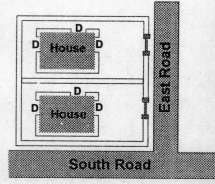

Q. Is it a Vaastu fault when a pole exists in the north-east direction, and there is also no wall in the east or north direction?

Ans. If a pillar exists in the north east direction, in that case walls must be built on both the sides of north and east, otherwise it constitutes a Vaastu fault. Moreover, both the walls should be in accordance with the road.

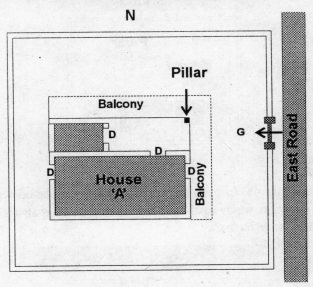

Note : In the above diagram even if the road exists in the east, there is no wall in the north-east direction, which is a Vaastu fault. In this context reference may be made to diagrams which follow here in after.

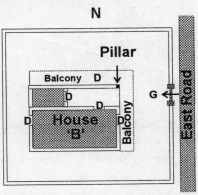

Note : In the above diagram a road lies to the east of the house, a wall has been erected in the northern side of north-east direction, because a pillar/pole is situated in north-east direction.

In diagrame 'c' the house is situated on the northern side of the road and there also exists a pole in the north-east direction. But, even then no wall has been built which is wrong Vaastu.

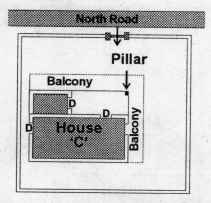

In the diagram 'D' (below) the house is situated in the northern side of north-west direction, where a pole also exists, but a wall has also been erected alongside the pole in the east.

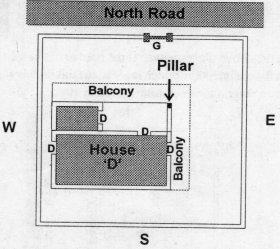

Q. Can the same person purchase plots which are located on both sides of the highway?

Ans. A person can purchase plots on both sides of the highway, provided the situation does not contravene Vaastu guidelines. Following diagram and related points should be taken into consideration, before any person opts to purchase a plot each on either side of the highway. In the diagram, given below, five plots have been earmarked on both sides of the highway.

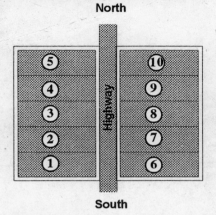

North

South

As shown in the above diagram, a person living at plot no. (1) can purchase plot no. 6, 7, 8, 9 and on the eastern side beyond the road / highway. Owner of plot no. 2 can purchase plots no. 7, 8, 9, 10, owner of plot no. 3 can purchase plot no. 8, 9 and 10, and owner of plot no. 4, Can purchase plot no. 9 and 10, but owner of plot no. 5, can purchase plot no. 10, Only.

If owner of plot no. 5, purchases plot nos 7, 8 and 9, such plots will not be useful as they are situated in the south-east direction. Similarly if owner of plot no. 4, purchases nos 6, 7, 8, it will also be inauspicious, owner of plot no. 3, should not purchase plot nos 7 and 6, Owner of plot no. 2, should not purchase plot no. 6.

Similary, a purchaser should not keep plots, on both sides of the road or highway, in the north-west or south-east sides. If the houses are situated in the north-east and south-west, results will not be identical.

Q. Till now facts about plot of land and obstruction of pathways have been explained. If such a situation surfaces / occurs directly from east, west, north and south direction, then how such situations can be avoided and remedied?

Ans. Road intrusion from east and west direction is auspicious which we call as extension on the north and east sides.

If intrusion occurs in the western side, a wall should be built in the house (as indicated in fig. 'A') to segregate the area — it will then become an extension and also be auspicious.

If the pathway intrusion occurs from the western side, such area should be segregated by erecting a wall (as shown in fig (c)). This way the intrusion will convert into an extension which will be an auspicious sign.

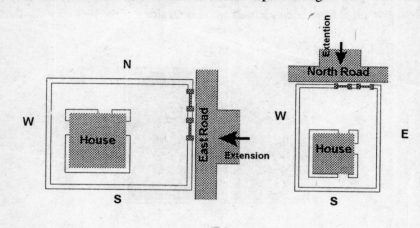

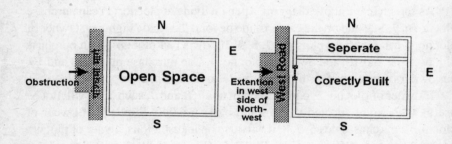

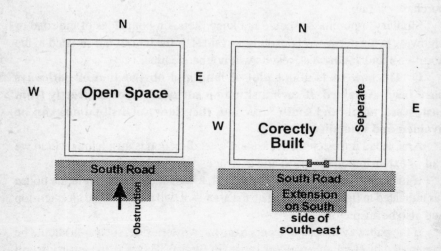

If space is found vacant in the north-west road, then divide the area as shown in the diagram.

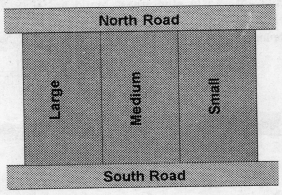

In case of the apartments, follow the indications, as given in the following diagram and divide the area.

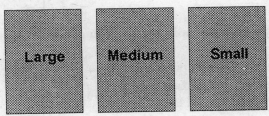

Q. Does Vaastu apply in the case of Government buildings also?

Ans. Government buildings are no exception to Vaastu rules, as the rules equally apply to all the buildings, whether they are owned by government or an individual.

Q. Where the electricity board and bulb be installed?

Ans. Electricity board can be install in any direction, except the north-east direction. But a bulb can be affixed in any place where it is actually required, but it must be ensured that the light falls on the back side from the left side.

Q. Which is the most suitable place for a 'Duplex'?

Duplex can be built in the north, east and in the north-east direction, as shown in the following diagram. But, it should never be built in the south, west and south-west direction, as it will yield ominous results.

Q. Does it not cause any fault, when godowns are built in the open sites?

Ans. Relevant Vaastu guidelines should be followed, while building godowns, as shown in the diagram hereunder.

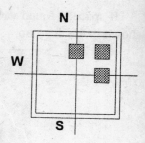

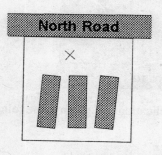

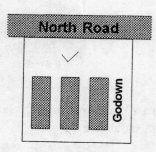

Q. Is it proper to build the house according to directional indicator / Compass?

Ans. When a road exists in the northern direction, then face the northern side, according the directional indicator and consturct a wall... it will extend the north-east, because a wall is built within the house. It is an auspicious sign. But, it will also cause extension of south side of south-east direction, western side of south-west direction and northern side of north-west direction—it will

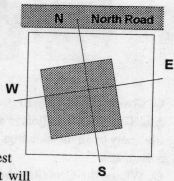

yield ominous results and effects. Hence, it is better if a house is built alongside the road. In the above diagram extension of 15⁰ space has been shown.

ii) If a road is situated in the north side, then construction should take place in the south and west (in line with the road) and eastern and northern sides should be slightly extended towards the north-east direction — this is how

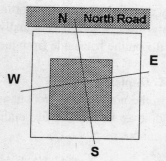

a house should be built. This rule or method will also apply to the houses, built in other directions, which have main gates.

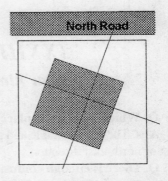

iii) If the road is situated in the north and the house has also a gate on the northern side and has also been built according to directional compass, it will result in extension towards the northern side of north-east direction, which is an auspicious sign. But it will cause odd extensions towards other directions also, viz extensions towards the eastern side of north-east direction, south side on the south-west direction, and western side of north-west direction—all the said extensious will yield only unfavourable results. Hence, it is always better to construct a house along the side of the road. In the diagram extension of 15⁰ degrees has been shown.

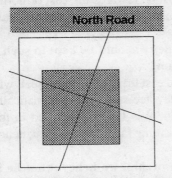

iv) House having main gate in the north, should not be built along northern side of the road, but should be built along the southern and western boundary wall, according to directional indicator, and also extend it slightly towards north and east sides of north-east direction—such type of construction is in order. These norms also apply to the houses which have main gates on other directions.

Q. When dwellers in a house or apartment wish to affect a division, which area should be occupied by each individual?

Ans. To begin with and as a first step, the members and partners in a house and or an apartment should sit together and express individual preference for a specific portion, but it must be as per laid down norms. If a road exists each on the east and west side of a dwelling unit, then the eldest partner / member should occupy the ground floor, the middle on the middle floor and the younger one the second floor, as shown in the diagram.

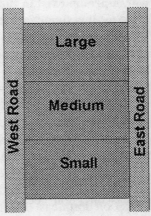

(XXIII) Worship Room
(Special hints about worship-room)

Q. Which is an ideal place for worship-room in the house?

Ans. The most suitable and ideal place for the worship-room in a house is east or north-east direction.

Q. There is enough confusion whether a devotee should sit in the east or north-east direction or he should face either of the sides? Please explain actual position.

Ans. As the Sun is a visible deity who is representative of omnipotent and omniscient almighty God, hence we should sit in the direction (east) from where the Sun rises. Moreover when we worship and offer water to the Sun we stand before the Sun. Hence our face must be towards the east or north-east direction. When we sit for worshipping, this important point which should be kept in mind while offering prayers.

Q. Some people opine that idol of the deity should be kept in such a way that it faces east or north-east direction?

Ans. If an idol of a deity is kept facing the east then, in such a case, it will be posited in the west side and also that the devotee's face will automatically be towards the western direction. If deity's idol is kept or installed in the north-west direction, then the devotee will be sitting facing south-west; hence both the said positions are wrong.

Q. Though we do not believe in idol worship. we believe that he is omnipresent, omnipotent and omniscient. In such a situation, should the worshiproom exist in the east or north-east direction?

Ans. It is simply a matter of individual faith and confidence whether you believe in God or not, as divine godly powers are not impacted by an individual's personal opinions and whims. Whether you have no faith or faith in the Sun, it continues to provide light and energy to all the living beings. But, it is necessary to know the mystical prowess of divine powers, as it adds to our knowledge, capability, even then our individual views have no effect on the powers of the Sun.

Further it is customary and matter of general courtesy and social behaviour that when we welcome and felicitate a person, we stand up facing him. It hardly matters whether we believe or not in the existence of the Sun. It is a proven reality that its endless energy can be had from it from the eastern corner on north-east direction. Even it has been proved scientifically that an

140

ideal and most suitable place for a worship room is only in the eastern side or north-east direction.

Our ancestors and ascetics were high grade scientists and truth seekers. The word 'Rishi' implies 'a person who continuously researches on truth and knowledge?, So, they are never wrong and our treatises are also never wrong. So, we should digest this stark reality with an open mind, before we start studying Vaastu science.

Atheism is a negative quality of a person and it is also thanklessness. A person is an atheist, if he does not belive in or demos a living reality and atheism has, so far, done no good to any person. If a person has complete faith in God and it's powers and divinity, then only he can imbibe nobel human qualities. His approach must be positive and fortified with a sense of gratitude.

Q. Most of the worship places are found in the kitchens? Is it in order?

Ans. such persons, who utilise their kitchens in the form of the worship place also, always remain tormented and sad, as their ancestors and deities are never pleased with them. As you already know that ancestors and deities appreciate feelings and fragrant essences. So, whatever items are cooked in the kitchen, release foul smell which is uncomfortable to all of them. Hence, they must not be treated in such a shabby way.

Q. Where should photos of ancestors be kept / hung?

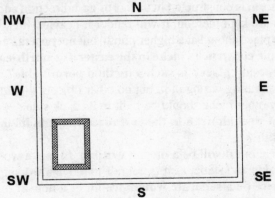

Ans. 1. Photos of dead ancestors should always be hung in the corner of south-west or in the western corner.

2. Heavy and unused articles should never be kept in the south-west corner.

2. Do not keep a dead ancestor's photo or picture in the worship room, as it will be placed alongwith idol of a deity, hence avoid the said situations. No doubt, our ancestors deserve our respect and faith, but they can neither be equated with nor substituted for our deities.

Q. Are not our ancestors worshippable like the dities? Then why their pictures can not be kept alongside idols or dities?

Ans. There is no person who can be equated with God. When a living person is not equal to God, then how can a dead person aquire such a status? After death, human body is simply a pack of earth, as all the five elements merge in the atmosphere. So, if we worship a dead person's soul, we are actually worshipping the souls of ghosts.

Our ancestors should always be given respect and shown gratitude for, without them, our existence was not possible. So, we should feel indebted to them and express our gratitude. Sometime, they attain divine qualities and powers and protect our house. Hence they are venerable. Despite all this, remember that they can neither be replaced nor even worshipped like the deities. Paying respects to our ancestors is not worship. If we worship them, our deties will get displeased.

So, photos or pictures of the ancestors can be hung in the west, south or south-west directons and respects paid to them and also worshipped, because such photos are not kept in the worship place. Some persons ignite earthen lamps at the places where water exits and then worship them- this is not a worship of the ghosts but the ancestors whose blessings will convert the everlasting energy into mystical powers.

Q. Some people construct a big platform in the north-east side and use it as worship place. Is it in order?

Ans. If a platform is constructed in the north-east direction and then idols and other objects are kept thereon, it will render it heavier. It is, however, a faith that worship place should at a higher plinth, but not on a raised platform.

Q. Some people construct a niche in the eastern or north-eastern wall and use it as a worship place? Is such a method permissible?

Ans. There is nothing wrong in it, but no other objects should be kept in it (niche), nor any other niche should be built in its back side.

Q. We have a steel almirah in the east direction, can its upper vault be used for worship?

Ans. Of course, but it will be a mobile worship. In fact a worship place should be immovable and static, as it is not fair to move a worship place.

Q. Should there be a separate worshiproom in a house?

Ans. If a person desires to aquire spiritual power and lusture, then his worship room must be separate and independent. When we can build separate children-rooms, bathrooms, dinning halls, bed rooms and drawing rooms, can't we build a separate room where we could worship peacefully and calmly? If we do not do so, it forebodes our stingly mentality. If it is not possible to build a separate worship room, a separate vault can, at least, be built in a room.

(XXIV) Holy Basil Plant

Q. What is the significance of Basil Plant in the context of Vaastu?

Ans. It is called 'Tulsi' or 'Ocymum Sanctum' also and is an extraordinary plant which has many therapeutic uses, hence it is also called a domestic physician. Vaastu is meant for the prosperity happiness and satiety of humanity, hence Holy Basil occupies an important place in Vaastu parlance, Housewives worship this plant as a deity and its medicinal properties and quality laden wind and water enhance and improve health. Even modern medical science has affirmed that dead bodies remain undecayed when kept in a holy Basil forest. It's contact and wind impart longer life and better health.

Holy Basil plant has many varieties, like 1) Shri Krishna Tulsi 2) Lakhshmi Tulsi 3) Rama Tulsi 4) Bhoo Tulsi 5) Neel Tulsi 6) Shweta Tulsi 7) Rakta Tulsi 8) Van Tulsi 9) Gyan Tulsi etc.

Due to its multiple medicinal uses, holy Basil occupies an important place in Ayurveda. It is hightly useful in diseases of ears, rose, throat, gastritis, flatulence, cough, fever, vomiting, heart diseases etc. If four holy basil leaves are ingested on empty stomach early in the morning, it will benefit in dialetes, blood deformities, bile, phlegm etc. If juice of holy basil leaves and lemon are mixed and dropped 3-4 drops in the painful ear, it will subside aural pain.

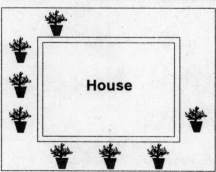

In fact, holy basil cures in almost all the diseases rather it is a panacea. It is an excellent remedy for malaria fever which (fact) was proved by Imperial Malaria Conference in 1907. Its leaves should be softened and applied over the site of scorpio-bite, it will remove the pain. It has been mentioned in

'Atharvaveda' that holy basil can convert an ugly face into a beautiful one.

Q. In which directions holy basil plant should be grown?

Ans. Holy basil plant can be planted in any house from the south side of south-west direction to the southern side of south-east direction, from western side of south-west direction to western side of north-west direction in the vacant area. Its plantform should be lower or higher than the central place of the house. If it is possible then erect a platform in the centre-part of house and its level should either be slightly lower or higher than the level of centre-part of the house. If it is not possible then build a platform in the north side of north-west direction in the centre-part of the house and its level should be lower than that of the centre-part, and then plant holy basil plant. Whichever option is adhered to, enough space must be left vacant all around the plant. If either of the said alternatives are not practicaly possible, then raise a platform at the centre point of the house, but keep in the level lower than that of the centre point, and then place holy basil pot or plant the bush.

If none of the foregoing proposals is feasible, then grow holy basil in earthen pot which should be kept in close proximity of western and southern walls but do not keep near east and northern walls. If this situation is also not feasible and there is no alternative but to keep the plant's earthen pot in the east or northern walls, then keep vacant space between eastern side of south-east direction and northern side of norht-west direction. But, all said and done, the best venue to keep the holy basil plant / earthen part is most benefic if kept in the centre-point of the house.

(XXV) Kithchen and Fire-Place
(Stove)

Q. Which is an appropriate place for the kitchen and a fire-place?

Ans. The most appropriate place for kitchen and stove is the corner of south-east, but a fire-place should not be made by carving a hole in the eastern wall because it will constitute a Vaastu fault, due to extension of eastern side of south-east direction. Even if a chimney is also provided for, entire house will be enveloped by smoke. Fire-place should be built in such a way that the cook's face remains towards the eastern side. See the following diagram for a practical view.

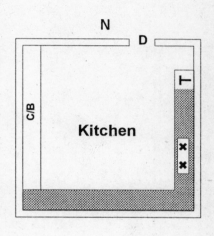

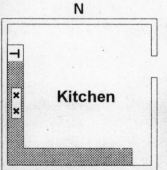

Q. If it is not feasible to keep a burner / stove in the south-east direction, then which is the other option?

Ans. In those houses, which have east-facing main gate, a burner should be kept in the south-west corner of the rooms which face north-west and south-west rooms.

Q. If it is not feasible to make provision for a fire place in the south-east corner of the houses, whose main gate is south-facing, then which is the other alternative?

Ans. Fire place should be provided for in the south-east corner of north-west room and the cook should cook food while he/she is facing the east direction, but oven, should not touch the northern wall - to make this proposal practical, erect a 1 ft. wide platform, three inches away from the wall. In addition, erect a wall three inches away from eastern side of south-east direction

145

and also construct a paltform from south and east walls to western side of north-east direction — this the place where a fire place can be provided for and a kitchen also built. Place underneath the platform should be kept open, fire—place should be towards west and cook should face eastern direction while cooking food. But, in any case, no niche should be made in the eastern wall in order to keep a stove.

(XXVI) Almirahs and Cash boxes

Q. On which sides should almirahs etc. be kept?

Ans. Almirah, sofa set, table or any other heavy material can be kept towards south and west sides of south-west direction. But it would be better if sofa, tables and chairs are placed in such a way that they touch southern and western walls.

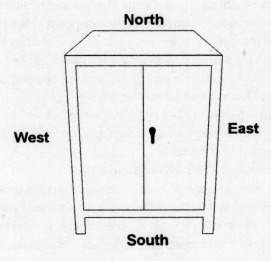

Q. In which side of the house cash box be kept?

Ans. Since valuable documents, gold, silver and cash are kept in a cash box, it should be keep in such a way that the same faces the northern side, as lord of wealth, Kuber, is the lord of northern direction. If you can ensure it, there will be no paucity of money.

A duly sanctified 'Kuber Yantra should be kept in the cash box. If on the festival of 'Dhan teras' Kuber yantra is worshipped (technically this process is called 'Shodashopachar), then there will be no dearth of wealth in the cash box. See the following diagram.

(XXVII) Feng Shui

Q. What is meant by the term Feng Shui?

Ans. It is a Chinese term which is like Indian Vaastu shastra. 'Feng' means 'Air' and 'Shui' means 'Water'. Hence Feng Shui means Air and water. These two elements are an integral part of chinese Feng Shui upon which this theory is based. These are nature's two elements whose power is used to make human life happy and prosperous. Some rules were formulated and applied by the chinese in respect of building construction and selection of a suitable piece of land for house building. These principles, concept and philosopy help us to understnd Feng Shui and its various facets.

Q. On which principles is Feng Shui based?

Ans. Feng shui is based on the concept of 1) Earth 2) Water 3) Fire 4) Metal 5) Wood and ten directions.

Q. How does Feng Shui affect human life?

Ans. Feng Shui casts indelible effect and imprint on a person's individual life, style of living, ways of eating, dining room, guest room, bed room, living room, interior and exterior decoration etc. If interior and exterior decoration, style of construction of a house are in consonance with those of the nature, then he enjoys excellent health, happiness, prosperity and comforts.

Q. How can Feng Shui or Vaastu science can help to improve our lot and daily life's problems?

Ans. If there is feud and altercation between wife and husband, house-owner does not make any progress, business is not profitable, there is absence of male progeny, there is mental tension in the family, there is unrest in the family, children do not study properly, children's progress is scuttled, some incurable disease manifests any family member, there is total absence of sleep, money is being wasted in court cases. In short nothing is in order. In the aforesaid situations, the affected person should contact an expert in Vaastu or Feng Shui and seek his guidance to improve conditions in the house and business enterprise and introduce requisite improvement to get rid of the said problems.

Q. To what extent can Feng Shui help to eradicate various deficiences and faults?

Ans. Feng Shui is capable of dispelling 50% of the deficiencies and faults and the rest of 50% is dispelled by a person's fate. In my opinion a person's horoscope, his fate, impact and movement of stars and phases should also be closely studied, in addition to Feng Shui, so that correct dignosis can be reached at. If Feng Shui faults are removed and hurdles to one's life, bad phases of stars are also removed, it will pave the way for cent percent favourable results.

Q. What gadgets or implements are used to dispel faults in Feng Shui?

Ans. These gadgets or devices can be classified as under:-

1. An octagonal Pakua Mirror.

2. Wind Chines.

3. Various pictures of Dragon.

4. Red Ribbon 5. Aquariun 6. Flutes 7. Three coins 8. Bunch of Flowers 9. Caligraplues 10. Crystal Ball 11. Lo-Shui 12. Bagua emulet (Yantra) 13. Various mystical Talismans 14. Tortoise 15. White Lion 16. Chinese compass 17. Red Bird.

Q. Has Feng Shui any relation with Religion?

And. Yes, their philosophy is based on the concept of "Ruist" and 'Taoism" which are integral parts of chinese Feng Shui. In fact chinese history starts from the methods to be used for burying the ancestors.

Q. Has Feng Shui any relation with Astrology?

Ans. Chinese astrology is part of Feng Shui. The chinese have great faith in lunar dates and lunar calendar and all their astrological calculations are based on these facets. They have paid great attention and significance as to whether a house should be built in a specific lunar month, direction from which side the entrance gate should exist and also which direction will be benefic and auspicious for a person who is born in a particular zodiac sign. So, if we do not fully understand and digest the astrology of the chinese, our knowledge about Feng Shui will remain incomplete and inconsistent.

Q. How does Feng Shui works?

Ans. The chinese believe that nature is manifested by a life force, which is an energy and it is a significant attribute and blessing of nature. It is called as 'Chi'. Hence, there must be a free and unhindered flow of 'Chi' in a home, house, shop, factory, industiral complex etc., so that there is continuos flow of energy in the built up buildings and if it so, it is a good Feng Shui, but a hindered and depleted flow of 'Chi' constitutes a bad Feng Shui. So, the Feng Shui experts initiate by ensuring free flow of life-giving energy (chi) in the house or factory, as the case may be.

Q. Which are the elements upon which 'Chi' is dependent?

Ans. Life-giving energy 'Chi' is dependent on two elements, viz 'YIN' and 'YANG'—Yin is a negative energy, while yang is a positive energy. In order to fully understand 'Chi', we have to first undersand yin and yang.

Q. What is menat by 'Yin' and where is its abode?

Ans. In a way, yin is the negative energy of nature and its abode is night, darkness and shadow. Its colour is black. Its abode is earth and it is more active and effective in cold and winter. Its abode is a hospital, mortuary and church. Its number is 'Z' hence it casts its impact on 2, 4, 6, 8, 10 numbers. Its favourite places are water, police station, cold colours, music, small windows, sentimental and emotive tendencies.

Q. What is meant by 'Yang' and where it has its abode?

Ans. In a way, it is nature's positive energy which resides in the heaven, the sun light, sharp light and fire. Its colour is white. It is more effective in spring and hot season. It occupies number '1' in numericals and numbers 1, 3, 5, 7 and 9 are impacted by it. It has its abode in temples of Goddesses, fire, generator, school, spiritual congregations & conferences, mantras. It has also its abode in beautiful flowers, plants, glittering objects, logical intellect and activity.

Q. Is Vaastu or Feng Shui effective only when a person has an abiding faith in it?

Ans. Vaastu science and Feng Shui are not dependent on one's confidence and faith. This science is based on five great elements and ten directions, which are scientifically proved facts. If a person has faith or not in this science, it hardly has any impact on this science. For instance, Sunlight and Sun-energy affects and benefits all human beings, species, poor, rich, Hindus, Muslims, Christians, Plants and trees, mountains etc. without any discrimination and it hardly matters even someone does not believe in the inherent life-energy or energy enshrined in sunrays and sunlight. So, it is hardly of any consequence whether same person has faith or no faith in solar energy, nor does it affect the Sun in any way whatsoever. Similarly, it also does not matter at all, if a person has or has no faith in Vaastu science, because effectivity of Vaastu will remain unaffected, as it is a perfect science and it works in its way. Discerning and intelligant persons derive gains from it, whereas those who are unintelligent, are like the brats, who live in the dark and abhor sunlight.

Q. Which are the main directions?

Ans. There are four main directions, viz.,

1) East 2) West 3) North and 4) South

Q. Which are the other directions and their names?

Ans. These are of four types viz. 1) North-east corner 2) South-east corner 3) South-west corner and 4) North-west corner. Foreign scholars combine the main four directions and sub-directions, and nomenclate them as four directions in all. But all the said directions and nomenclations are based on Indian research and the foreignrss also concede this fact.

Q. How many directions does Indian Vaastu science recognise?

Ans. Indian Vaastu science recognised eight directions and eight 'Dikpals' (deity or lords who control these directions). The eight directions are as follows:-

1. East 2. West 3. North 4. South

5. South-east 6. South-west 7. North-west and 8. North-east 9. Sky and 10. Underground

Q. Are there any other directions, in addition to the above mentioned directions?

Ans. According to ancient Indian treatises there as 24 directions, in addition to the ones described herotofore.

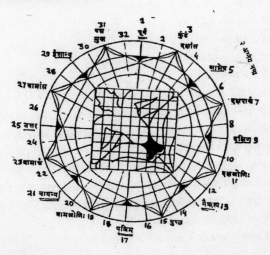

151

It is known as Dus Dishas Dikpal Bodhak Chakra

Details given in the above diagram are detailed hereunder.

Direction	Lord	Weapon	Vehicle	Colour of direction
1. East	Indra	Vajra	Elephant	Yellow
2. West	Varun	Paash	Fish	Smoky
3. North	Kuber	Gada	Horse	Golden
4. South	Yama	Dand	He/Buffalo	Black
5. Norht-east	Eesh/Rudra	Trishul	Bull	Red
6. South-east	Fire	Shakti	Rain	Red
7. South-west	Nariti	Kharag	Lion	White
8. North-west	Wind	Goad	Deer	Black
9. Upper/Sky	Brahman	Begging bowel	Swan	White
10. Lower/ Underground	Anant/ Vishnu	Wheel (Chakra)	Eagle	Yellow

Q. What are the names of lords of directions?

Ans. Please refer to the above classification.

Q. Does Feng Shui also believe in the concept of directional lords, as the Vaastu shastra does?

Ans. Feng Shui recognises only four directions and directional Lords, viz.

1. East direction — its lord is Dragon
2. West direction — its lord is white Tiger
3. North direction — its lord is Black Turtle
4. South direction — its lord is Feng Huang

Q. Is Feng Shui science or an Art?

Ans. Feng Shui dates back to 5000 years from now. It is based on chinese beliefs, traditions and concepts, upon which is based the concept of house building, the art of living life. But its concept of dragon and its worship aligns this science to blend worship. Moreover, their concept and philosophy of five elements includes elements like metal and wood reveals their lack of understanding and unscientific approach. There are many other such contents which compel us not to recognise Feng Shui in the category of science and we can not call it an art also, in technical term.

Q. Is Indian Vaastu a science or an art?

Ans. Indian Vaastu Shastra has two aspects, viz. a purely religious aspect and another a purely scientific aspect. Purification of land, ceremony for foundation laying, installation of building, worship and recitation of hymns/verses from scriptures, Vaastu sacrifice come under the purview of religious aspect—it can also be called the 'later part of Vaastu' which invariably includes, among other things, various yantras (emulets), recitation of mantras and worship and dispelling of Vaastu related faults and directions.

Earlier part of Vaastu, which relates to the great five elements and ten directions, is a cent-percent science. So, Vaastu has both the religious and scientific aspects.

Q. Should Indian Vaastu shastra's religious aspect be deemed as an unscientific aspect?

Ans. Boundaries of spirituality start from where the scientific limits end. Hence second part of Vaastu shastra should not be deemed on a weak leg. Many Instances can be quoted where Vaastu faults and deficiencies were miraculously eradicated by worship, recitation of mantras and religious observances.

Q. Can you cite some examples when people benefitted by resorting to adoption of Vaastu scinece?

Ans. There are innumerable examples when people immensely derived advantage by resorting and adopting the golden principles of Vaastu, which resulted in complete transformation of their life, but most of such people do not disclose their names. It is like asking a doctor of a busy hospital to cite the names of cured persons which is a complex problem, as innumerable persons get cured through medical treatment, hence it is neither possible to tell their names, publish relevant records, nor it is wise and useful. Of cousre percentage of cured cases may be disclosed, as truth needs no proof. If you scruplously follow Vaastu rules, you can yourself see the miracles, and on the basis of my own experience that cent-percent success is possible.

In this context I will relate an unforgettable example. In 1996, I visited a hospital in residential town of Industrial city, Kanpur, in U.P. and paid a Vaastu visit. There were ten storeys opposite each other, and there was one house plan and same design, mensuration and elevation were also identical. There was an operation theatre, lift, consultation rooms for patients and a drug shop on each of the floors, in between each floor. There were ten residential storeys opposite each other where hospital's trustee, specialist and other doctors and various prominent persons had purchased residential flats. But, one problem had been haunting residents in one storey where all persons were poor, miserable, unhappy and afflicted and none of the residents had any progeny. One of the floors was situated in the northern side and the other in the south direction, but the host of problems were faced by the people residing in the southern side. When these persons came here they were happy and prosperous, but all of whom became afflicted, pennyless and defunct; so they sold out their flats at much lower rates. Some NRIS also purchased flats here but their financial condition started to deteriorate and their general condition also worsened. Some couples had only one son and they wanted to pass their retired life and old age comfortably and peacefully, hence they purchased flats here. In the case of a couple, their only son fell ill but he could not survive despite being attended by specialist and competent doctors of private nurshing home, where all the modern medical facilities were available. There were also examples of this sort and gradually it became a talk of the town that all the south-facing flats and storeys were ominous and afflicted.

When modern cosmic science failed to yield any fruitful outcome, then it was thought fit to seek remedy under the guidance of Vaastu experts, spiritual and religious persons. There are two types of Vaastu experts—one type are theists while the others are atheists. Thaist Vaastu scholars have faith in the existence of God. Religion, meditation, worship, recitation, soul etc., whereas the atheist Vaastu scholars consider Vaastu a science of limited approach and find it in water light compartments. They consider, religion, worship. adherance to Vaastu concept, religious ceremonies, rituals etc. a humbug. They laid more stress on compass and modern instruments and wished to be called as Engineers, or still better as Vaastu Engineers as such titles inflate and boost up their ego. Such pseudo and self styled, self-approbated Vaastu Engineers have no knowledge of Sanskrit language and Indian treatises. Vedic Vaastu is alien to their comprehension. But they can fluently speak English, will talk (talk only) about biorhythm, magnetic, but only in theory. Such type of Vaastu engineers did visit the hospital, but could not make out any thing about the real malady which had afflicted the inmates of those storeys.

The chief trustee and the sufferers came to know about my address and they contacted on phone and fax., and sent house-plan. On seeing the house plan I, at once, located the basic malady, but they insisted on my Vaastu visit. So, I reached Kanpur where I was accorded a hearty welcome by the trustees, all the doctors and other renowned dignatories.

There was not much variation in the building plan and practical construction and the malady was the same of which I had already apprised them, hence solution was also the same. As they had immense faith and reverence for me,

154

they wanted that I should personally visit all the areas which were afflicted. I dug in 'Krityanashak Vaastu Yantra' in the earth, performed Vedic Vaastu Yagya (Sacrifice) with the help of local Vedic scholars. Remedial steps taken by me showed instantly miraculous results within three days, as all the Vaastu and other faults got dispelled within three days, but a modern educated person will not readily believe in my achievement, as they have shallow knowledge only.

Our discerning and intelligent readers would certainly want to know as to what was Vaastu fault that existed in the hospital which played such havoc. Now I explain the crux of the problem. In both the northern and southern storeys elevation, number of rooms, mensuration, toilets, drawing rooms and kitchen were identical. There was also identical arrangement for light, air, water, sunlight, doors and windows were also identical and there was not even an iota of variation. But the directions had got changed which fact was beyond the comprehension of so called Vaastu engineers and Feng Shui experts. All the toilets in the northern storey were built in the south-west direction, and when the same type of toilets were built in the southern storey, the same automatically were located in the north-east direction. Vedic Vasstu Science cousiders north and East sides as sacred direction. Sacredness can only be maintained and sustained when there is presence of a permanent worship room, a prayer room, place for yoga and meditation, daily use of essences and fragrances and auspicious pictures of deities. Hence no toilet or urinal should even be built in these two directions, failing which these directions become defiled and unholy. In such houses family lineage does not prosper, children are immoral, fame, name, prosperity and wealth come to an end—this what happened at Kanpur. Earlier I had advised them to change the site of toilet through my letter. Persons, who know me know that I do not believe in wear and tear of house to remove Vaastu faults. I have also written book, entitled Remedial Vaastu (In Hindi and translated in English) which is sold like hot cakes. But there are certain situations where one can not and must not compromise and in this case, toilets had to be removed, as it was the only viable solution and remedy. Other situations can be remedied and corrected without wear and tear and by installation of Dikdoshanashak Yantra, Vaastu Managalkari Yantra, Vaastu Mangal Kari toran, Vaastu doshnashak Ganpati etc.

Even minor Vaastu faults can play havoc of immense magnitude. Here I would refer to an incident that upset the life of a businessman of Delhi, who knew me for the past ten years and is like my disciple. He built a palatial bungalow in Rohini enclave, Delhi. He got house plan approved by me and I

155

laid foundation stone of his house. Five Vedic scholars from Jodhpur performed installation, purification of land, awakening of land, and Vaastu Yagya (Sacrifice) as per Vaastu directions. When the house was ready, for inaugural entry, he got the relevant rituals and practices performed by the Vedic scholars of Delhi, as I had already proceeded on a foreign tour. He was a thiest and a noble industrialist, who performed all the laid down procedures.

The moment he entered his new house, he became more wealthy and prosperous, as his business progressed by leaps and bounds, but unusual problem surfaced, as he could not sleep, at all, at night. Despite all possible treatment sleep evaded him, as he became mentally tense, saw frightful dreams which caused him restivity. Tired and reluctant, he used to go to his factory but, when he returned, he was an exhausted and weak person. He used to watch T.V. upto 12 at night, read books but sleep still eluded him. So, his physical problem added to his business related problems and anxities. All these upsets adversely impacted his health and he became hypertensive, his blood pressure also raised. Now both the husband and wife contacted me on phone and complained that, if every Vaastu related rules have been complied, why such a problem should have surfaced. When health is in disorder, no religious beliefs can help. So, I squeezed out some time from my awfully busy schedule and reached Delhi. I was amazed to realize that his entire family had great regards for me, despite problems, they accorded me a hearty welcome. When I entered I was required to inspect and watch closely every hook and corner of their house. I was flabbergasted to see the grandeur of interior decoration, costly furniture and all other articles. When I observed and inspected every aspect minutely, I noticed that the fact was exactly posited towards the chest of a sleeping person. There was replica of a wooden snake on one side and black cobra on the other side. It seemed as if the black cobra would bite by raising its hood. There was a large mirror on the side of the bed, because the businessman was a amorist who felt delighted when saw himself and his wife while mating. I should not refer to this personal aspect, but I would certainly like to point out some glaring facts about his bedroom which I would like to share with my readers.

1. There should be no pictures of birds and ferocious animals in the bedroom.
2. There should be no sexy photos / pictures in the bedroom nor any other odd pictures.
3. No fan, lamp shade, electric bulb or tube should be fixed in such a way that it comes over the sleeping person.
4. No looking mirror, piece of reflective glass should be kept or fixed in a

bedroom where a person can see his own body and it hardly matters whether the glass used is black or white.

5. Walls in the bed-room should never be painted with any dark or black colour.

6. Do not convert the bedroom into a store house, by dumping useless and unwanted articles therein.

7. Bedroom should never be used as a worshiproom and no worship material or pictures or photos of dead persons (ancestors) should be kept in a bedroom.

8. Do not keep any blue film, porno casettes, obscene books, liquor bottles, detective novels in the bedroom, as all of them will cast adverse impact on the yet-to-be born children.

9. If you want to lead a happy life, retire to bed at 10.00 P.M. and get up between 5-6 A.M.

10. Do not attend late night parties and dinners. Take your dinner immediately after sun set to keep your digestive system in perfect order. If you do so, you will not get up as a tired person, rather you will feel refreshed and relaxed.

11. If you suffer from chronic or recent complaint of insomnia / sleeplessness or even disturbed sleep), rinse your face, hands and feet before retiring to bed and leave aside all your anxieties and problems. You can also recite 'Ratri Sookta' before retiring to bed or place the 'Swapan Vinashak Yantra' underneath your pillow, which had been specially prepared by our office to remove insomnia.

Amen! So, you must have followed the factors which were impedimental factors in causing insomnia to the said businessman. Actually, there was nothing wrong according to Vaastu rules, but interior decoration, articles kept in a room (say bed-room) converting your bedroom into a store house, photos or pictures of dead persons, canine birds, ferocious animals, dark paint of walls, obscene books, porno movies and cassettes, detective novels etc. should never be kept in any bedroom, due to the reasons mentioned above. So, I removed all the anomalies and undesrable articles from the bedroom and imparted orderliness to his bedroom. After all the corrective and remedial measures, the said gentleman started enjoying sound sleep. So, it must be borne in mind that correct Vaastu is not enough, interior decoration and all other requisite measures are also equally significant. But a layman can not detect all the anomalies hence guidence of an experienced Vaastu scholar is of prime importance.

You should seek Vaastu advice and guidance from only one Vaastu expert, but if you go on seeking guidance from many experts, you will get perplexed, hence do not go on changing Vaastu experts every now and then, rather stick to only one (after making a judicious choice) expert only and follow his guidelines and directions. There is an old maxim that 'To many cooks spoil the broth' which equally applies in case of Vaastu experts also.

There is another instance in this context which pertains to Agra City. Where an industrilist built a house under my Vaastu guidelines. When I returned to Agra again he, following an engineer's advice, got fixed all the walls at and near the main gate, fixed with granite tiles. As a rule no granite tiles should be used on the main gate and other walls, as it destroys name and fame of the house owner. When sunrays fall upon granite tiles they reflect on the Sun, resulting in autogonisation of lord Sun who punishes the owner and destroys his reputation. So, there was a raid at the premises of the said businessman who was jailed also.

There are numerous instances on this subject and if I refer to all of them, even volume of a book will not suffice to include all my experiences in this regard, rather I may have to write a separate book on 'Vaastu experiences'. What I want to actually impress up is this Vaastu science comes handy in our daily life, as it is a practical science and if the laid down guidelines and rules are followed in entirety, it will result in instant favourable results. There is no scope for suspecting utility of Vaastu science nor is there gain in closing our eyes to realities and if someone opts to venture in this regard, he will simply display his idiocy and lack of proper knowledge.

(XXVIII) Interior Decoration

Q. What is implied by the term Interior/Internal Vaastu?

Ans. The Chinese believe that our physical health, thinking and mental equilibrium are greatly impacted by the environments that exist around us. If a person resides in an oddly built house, his mental, physical and intellectual behaviour will also be odd.

Paint or colours used in interior portion of a house, provision for light and air, interior decoration immensely affect 'Q' of a house and in turn, life and behaviour of the inmates of the house, get also automatically impacted. For instance, too many and too heavy furniture articles obstruct free flow of 'Q'. Any person, living in such a choked and overloaded room, will feel restive and his health will also be downward, for the simple reason obstructed life force casts ill impact on a resident's internal life force and 'Aura'. Conversely, in a room, which only has minimal furniture and other articles, there will be full and unobstructed flow of 'Q', due to which the resident will also enjoy a healthy and sound body and mind. Hence, we can say that there must be proper balance between 'Q' and underground 'Q'. Internel 'Q' of a house can be controlled by interior decoration, and study of this facet is called 'Internal / interior Vaastu. According to this theory we affect interior decoration in such a way that flow of 'Q' remains intact without any hindrance. So, there must be an interrelation between underground (subterraniean) energy and internal 'Q' of a house.

Q. What's your opinion about interior decoration?

Ans. Interior decoration, style of construction of a house is clearly indicative of a person's character, taste, preference, mental attitude and thinking, imagination and objectives. For instance, when we enter an unknown person's house, we can at once, guess about his orderliness, arrangement of things and his life-style as per the conditions discernable through interior decoration and articles. If interior decoration is found odd, it means the house owner is also oddly placed and mentally disturbed and his life is also disorderly, and that he is passing his life under tyring and painful situations. Conversely if the interior decoration plan is in perfect order, then house-owner's life will also be orderly, happy and peaceful and he will be also peaceful and happy. Hence interior decoration is a mirror of a person's life-style and his life in general. It may also be borne in mind that colours used within the house, cleanlines and general hygiene arrangement for water, sitting arrangement, size of furniture, pictures hanging on the walls greatly cast their impression on a house owner's life and activities.

Water is considered a symbol of wealth, hence artificial fountains can be built in the house so as to let in and enhance wealth.

By improving the interior decoration of a house, its Vaastu can also be improvised. So, we can resort to take to the following measures to improve Vaastu in a building, without wear and tear.

1. Mirror / Glass.
2. Sharp Lights.
3. A bell having a musical sound.
4. Trees and bunches of flowers.
5. Crystal ball.
6. Aquarium.
7. Water ponds and fountains.
8. Heavy electrical appliances / gadgets.
9. Heavy weight idols.
10. Flutes and Bamboos.

In addition to the measures, suggested above, all the articles should be kept at proper and designated places. For instance, electrical appliances should be kept in the south-east corner, water related articles in the north-east, heavy domestic articles in the south-west corner and then resort should be had to interior decoration—this is how internal Vaastu can be improved, so that it could prove fruitful and auspicious for the house owner.

All the cosmetics, useful articles, art pieces should be kept and used at appropriate places. Use maximum numbers of glass in the house, pay more attention to cleanliness and light, so that semen of a native is strong and potent. It will also add to his fortune and general well-being.

If colours used in a house are in conformity with planetary position of the native, it will not only be auspicious but fruitful also. Following details about a native's dominant element, his zodiac sign and which colours should be used, on the walls of houses, buildings, hotels, shops etc.

Native's dominant Planet	Zodiac Sign	Ascendant	Suitable Colours
1. **Sun**, posited in	Leo	Leo	Golden Yellow,

exalted sign, lord of its own sign or in a benefic and favourable position			golden border, light pink or yellow
2. Dominant **Moon** element, Moon lord of its own house, exalted	Cancer	Cancer	Milky White, White, silver colour and decoration with silver colour
3. **Mars** dominant, posited in Aries, Scorpio or Capricorn Zodiac Sign	Aries Scorpio	Aries Scorpio	Orange red, Crimson red, Coral red
4. **Mercury** Favourable position and benefic	Gemini	Gemini	Green Colour rooms
5. **Jupiter** effects powerful	Sagittarius, Pisces	Saggitarius Pisces	Light Yellow, Cream, Golden Yellow
6. **Venus**	Taurus Libra	Taurus Libra	Diamond White, Cream
7. **Saturn** Lord of its own house in exalted position, more effective in virgo	Capricorn Aquarius	Capricorn Aquarius	Sky blue
8. Rahu (Dragon's tail)	—	—	Smoky Colour, Multi-Colours
9. Ketu (Dragan's head)	—	—	Brown, Grey

Colour planning and interior docortion will yield benefits, favourable results and also remove Vaastu faults which are caused by stars and constellations

(Nakhshatras). Hence, while building a house, factory, shop, office also, always ensure that above mentioned points, viz. planetary positions and Vaastu faults, are also taken into consideration while deciding for choice of interior decoration and colours.

Removal of Vaastu faults without any wear and tear

Q. How can Vaastu faults be amended and corrected without any wear and tear?

Ans. Actually this is a corrective, curative remedial approach by which Vaastu faults can be dispelled without wear and tear. Prof. Leun has suggested new 'Cures' to dispel Vaastu faults by establishing equilibrium with space, fire, light and earth, in his book entitled 'NINE BASIC CURES' which are detailed hereunder.

1. Light — Mirror, Crystal Ball.
2. Sound — Bell.
3. Plants, Trees, Bushes, Flowers.
4. Wind-Mill, Fountain, Compass.
5. Idols, Stones, Rocks.
6. Various electrical appliances.
7. Colour Planning
8. Bamboo
9. Various emulets, yantras

If the aforesaid measures are taken, it will help to eradicate various 'aastufaults.

Q. Some of the corrective and specific measures may be suggested so that Vaastufaults are corrected without resorting to any wear and tear.

Ans. Nine corrective and remediel measures have been spelled out above in this context which are more popular methods. There are, in addition, other four methods which can also be undertaken for the same purpose.

(XXIX) Utility and use of Various articles

Q. What are the other Four Methods?

Ans. The four methods are detailed hereunder.

1. Use, utility and significance of Glass / Mirror

Mirror holds an important position in correcting some Vaastu faults. It is maintained that (the bigger the mirror, the better.) Mirror is more useful in offices and business premises, as mirror enhances and adds to fame, wealth and prosperity. Mirror should be installed in such a way that full reflection of a person could be easily seen in it. If size of a mirror is small and head is not reflected and seen in the mirror, it will cause headache to the house owner. But, if the mirror is too large, it will cause ill health to the house owner. It is also important that a mirror is posited at an appropriate place.

In a small and narrow room, faces will look beautiful and doubly sized. If a mirror is fixed or kept in an office, it will help to define and denote reflection, entrance and purpose of an incoming visitor. In an L-Shaped house or room a mirror is kept or fixed at an appropriate place, it will help greatly in enhancing prosperity and progress.

Sun-rays and sunlight get reflected in the mirror. Crystal ball is a source of positive energy and it despels internal and external Vaastu faults in a house and office. Any crystal is capable of reflecting sunrays first and then create rainbow colours. Hence, crystal ball improves the fate of a house owner by means and help of rainbow colours. There exist glaring variables in the use of a mirror and crystal ball, viz a mirror will only cast its impact only in a specific direction, whereas a crystal ball spreads its salutary and benefic effect in all the directions. A mirror has the property of dispelling damaging impact of external Vaastu faults only, hence its size holds no significant importance.

2. What is the significant role of bright light of a bulb in Feng Shui context?

Ans. Bright light is a significant tool to improve Vaastu related faults, as it improves environment also. It also converts an L-Shaped house to a square one. If a house is built at the slop of a mountain and when light is thrown on its frontal portion, it will stop incoming wealth. Bright light represents sunlight which brightens the internal and external form of a house. A person can get horrified by evil spirits, ghosts and other such forms in darkness. Moreover, darkness causes ill fortune, misery, pain and remorse, whereas light is representative of good fortune, prosperity and happiness. It is said :

"Brighter the lamp, better the Fate."

According to Vaastu principles divine powers reside and remain awakened in a house while light remains permanently in the east or north-east direction of a house.

3. Q. What is implied by melodious musical waves or wind-chirres? and how they function?

Ans. Sweet and melodious musical sounds or waves and modern bells are competant dispellers of bad omens due to generation of positive energy in a house or an office, in addition to removing Vaastu faults. Such devices or gadgets are fixed at the main gate so that the bells start ringing automatically whenever any unknown person enters in a house or office. Use and prevalence of this system of bells in the Reserve Bank of India, in fact, is the contribution of a Vaastu expert.

4. Q. What is the utility of 'Fish-Bowls' in Feng Shui?

Ans. Fish-bowls are also a source and symbol of natural beauty, like trees, plants and vegetations, as they also impart life-force and life-energy. When there is dearth of water element in a house or office, then the deficiency of this element is compensated by fish-bowls so as to remove and modify Vaastu defects. Hence, fish bowls are used to prevent misfortunes in a house or office. As soon a fish dies, it should be, at once, replaced by another live fish-.Bubbles arising in a fish-bowl are symbols of life-force and energy and they also give the impression of fountains which pave the way for prospertiy and happiness.

Q. Why Feng Shui recommends use of water sources like Fountains and Aquariums?

Ans. Water sources like Aquariums and fountains are recommended for use in big mansions, hotels, multi-storeyed buildings, commercial complex shops etc. to eradicate Vaastu faults, in an orderly manner. Water is the symbol of life, as it pacifies and cools eyes, keeps mind overjoyed, removes external heat present in the weather, creates moisture and mollifies internal restivity of mind, satiates thirst and impacts mental tranquility.

Water is considered as symbol of wealth in Central Asia and Air as the symbol of life itself. So, this way, Feng Shui means 'Water and Air' element and to enhance wealth by means of water and Air, Similarly, fountains and other water sources are also indicative of income.

Q. What is the significance of Bamboo and Flutes in Feng Shui?

Ans. It is a firm conviction of Feng Shui Vaastu Science that flutes, made of bamboo, impart peace, bring good and favourable news, permanency and stability. Hence, flutes are installed in offices, homes, business premises. It is believed that if one flute is placed upon another, in proximity to the holes, it will protect each storey in a built up structure.

Two flutes are couched in a red piece of cloth and kept in a triangular shaped device, protect a house or building from the beams and related hazards, so as to mollify beam related Vaastu faults. But, it may be kept in mind that face of the flutes should be downward. Use of flutes forebodes progress, prosperity, increase in positive qualities etc. In residential house, it is hung and decorated like a sword so that wicked souls, theives, dacoits and other bad persons are not able to cause any harm to the house and its inmates. According to religious beliefs when a flute is moved with a hand, then evil spirits take to their heels and when it is played, then auspicious magnetic flow enters the house.

Q. What is implied by Feng Shui and where is it more famous?

Ans. Chinese Feng Shui is a counterpart of Indian Vaastu, hence it can be called as chinese Vaastu Science. It is a combination of two words, that is air and water, hence literally Feng Shui means a 'Science of air and water' but its import (talent meaning) being. (A science which helps to increase accumulation of wealth in a house through air and water? In Feng Shui earth's magnetic power is divided into two magnetic powers of the earth, viz.

1. Dense underground energy — YANG
2. Underground Energy — YIN

The Chinese Vaastu (Feng Shui) experts locate these underground energies with the help of 'Luopan'.

As the earth has its underground magnetic energy, so has every person its own magnetic waves in his body. According to Chinese beliefs such energies are called by the name of 'Qi'. As 'Qi' imparts correct knowledge, intelligence, strength, physical capacity to a human body, so does earth 'Qi' help a person to attain success in worldly and spiritual development. Feng Shui is a secret arc to search out this talent 'Qi', and it hardly matters whether this 'Qi' is present in one room, entire building, hotel complex or piece or plot of land.

Scope of Feng Shui

According to Chinese belief the atmosphere around us casts its impact on our physical health, thought process and mental equilibrium. For instance, following instances may suffice to prove our point.

1) Effect of Construction of a house

If a construction of any building is odd, on a narrow piece of land or is uneven (disorderly), the mind and intellect of the residents will also be odd and misplaced.

1) Colour of building

Colour painted in a building, interior decoration and arrangement for proper air and light affect the resident's mental waves. If our room is painted with a dark and heat generating colour, the person sitting in such a room, will feel restive and charged with heat, conversely if colour of painting is light and also generates coolness, the person sitting in such a room will experience peace and coolness.

Hence much attention, on a building's interior decoration, internal construction style, has been paid in Feng Shui, as internal (interior) construction and decoration of a house or building denote the dweller's character, choice, preference, mental thoughts, imaginations and objectives.

Q. What is the aim of Feng Shui?

Ans. Aim of Feng Shui lies in attaching greater importance to size and shape of a plot upon which a house is to be built, style and technique of construction alongwith interior decoration, furniture, pictures, curtains and decoration articles so that a proper balance can be maintained between 'Qi' of the land and buildings internal Qi. Proper equilibrium between the said (two) types of Qi is responsible for maintaining proper balance in respect of underground and interior construction in the context of residential houses, apartments, shops, offices, hotels, gardens, factories, industrial houses, commercial complexes etc.

Peculiar Feature of Feng Shui

Feng Shui is Chinese Vaastu Science. They construct artificial water resources, like waterfalls, at the main gates so that money flows unobstructed as water is a symbol of wealth for them. Southern direction is kept more decorated and well maintained. The purpose behind this practice is to install flow of wind from Mangolia from the northern direction. Hence, they provide for more windows in northern direction and close such windows.

Differences between Feng Shui and Vaastu Science

Q. What are the basic differences between Chinese Feng Shui and Indian Vaastu Science?

Ans. In this context following variable points need to be mentioned.

1) Literal meaning of Feng Shui is water and air but its latent meaning (allegorcial meaning) is to establish proper equilibrium between nature's energy sources and man's life.

2) Whereas in Vaastu nature's five great elements, like water, air, earth, fire and space, are considered nature's inherent attributes. Entire universe

and human physical body (etheral body) is composed of the said five elements and existence of universe and the human beings is dependent upon these elements. But in Feng Shui Earth, Water, Fire, Metal and Wood have been accorded much importance and this science revolves around these basic factors (elements).

3) Land purification, land worship, land digging, laying of foundation have been dealt with in details, whereas these aspects are totally missing in Feng Shui.

4) Vaastu refers to four main types of earthen soil and 154 of types of land, but Feng Shui considers only yellow and red soil suitable for construction of buildings.

5 & 6) According to Vaastu disposal of natural water is considered best in the north-east and northern directions and is also considered as a source of comforts, wealth and luxuries but this aspect finds no place in Feng Shui which accords no importance to water and slope of the land but considers presence of water or a fountain at the main door (entrance gate).

7) According to Indian Vaastu Science, there should be optimum number of windows on the north direction while Feng Shui considers this (northern) side as ominous and directs that windows should be in the south than the north.

8) Indian Vaastu recommends building of kitchen in the south-east direction and also suggests keeping of heavy electrical equipments in this direction but these rules are alien to Feng Shui which directs storing of such material only in this direction.

9) According to Feng Shui north direction is considered as a meeting place for the soul and also for spirituality but Indian Vaastu considers north side as the direction of lord of wealth (Kuber).

10) Feng Shui considers north-east direction as ominous and unsacred and no window is built in this direction whereas Indian Vaastu Science considers north side as the most sacred direction, as lord of this direction is lord Eesh, and it is the place from where maximum volume of sacred energy is released.

11) Feng Shui recommends use of mirror, crystal ball, wind chimes, picture of dragon, octagonal mirror, fish-bowl etc. to dispel Feng Shui and Vaastu faults, while Indian Vaastu science lays stress on resorting to various types of yantras, Ganpati's yantras, sacrifice, oblation, purification of land etc. to remove Vaastu related faults.

12) Hereunder is given a comparative list of colours and the traits attributed to each colour in Vaastu Science and Feng Shui.

Indian Vaastu Science	Colour	Chineses Feng Shui
Symbol of Mars, War, Fire, Anger	Red	Strength and Courage
Represents Jupiter Sign Spirituality,	Yellow	Metal element
It is an ominous colour, is representative of Saturn	Blue	Sanguineness
Peace and Coolness	White	Peace, happiness, Yang Energy
Renewed Strength, aspiration	Orange	Happiness
Death	Black	Yin energy
Represents Smoke, Suspicion	Grey	Proportion
—	Purple	Respect
Represents Ketu	Brown	Anxiety, earth element

13) Before building a house horoscopes of the proposed building and its owner are compared in Vaastu Shastra and effect of the building on the owner's life is also determined, but in Feng Shui this aspect is missing.

14) Art of construction of a temple, sculpture, architecture and art of masonary are integral part of Indian Vaastu Science, but such aspects remain untouched in Feng Shui.

15) In ancient times redemption of direction was meant to erect a place for performance of sacrifice as per directions of Vaastu Science. The sacrifices were performed for world peace, without any discrimination of sex, caste, geographical limits and countries, as the ultimate aim was welfare of all the living species in the universe. 'सर्वे भवन्तु सुखिनः' which implies universal welfare, whereas Feng Shui is centered around individual gains and for a particular country only, for a specific civilization. Hence approach of Indian Vaastu Science is universal but that of Feng Shui is purely individual.

16) Indian Vaastu Science attaches great importance to the Sun, who it considers as deity who bestows energy to all the beings. As Sun rises in the east, so east and north-east directions are considered pious, as they impart life-gaining energy. Hence, it has been forbidden to build any

toilet or even keep shoes in the said directions, whereas in Feng Shui. Dragon is considered as the lord of eastern direction, tortoise in the north and west directions, and white lion of the southern direction. The Chinese also believe that bad omens and ill effects can be dispelled if pictures of such animals are dangled / affixed on relevant directions — it will also safeguard the inmates from direction of faults, according to Feng Shui.

17) According to Indian Vaastu Science there are eight directions and each one has its own lord (or incharge, such as Indra in the east, Varun in the west, Yama in the south, Kuber in the north, Eash in north-east, Agni in the south-east, Wind in the north-west, Brahman in the upward direction, and there are many deities in the underground portion of earth. These (directional) deities installed and worshipped with mantras so as to seek emancipation from directional faults. Recitation of mantras generates energy, and prayers and mantras induce godly powers to convert negative energy into positive energy. All those beliefs are shared by all the civilizations of the world excepting, of course, Feng Shui and the Chinese. There is however, no place for recitation of mantras, worship etc. in Feng Shui.

18) Vaastu-Purush's concept has been introduced in Indian Vaastu Science wherein land is divided into nine parts and door-planning is adhered to according to Vaastu-Purush (Vaastu Personified), whereas in Feng Shui an instrument is used for the same purpsoe.

19) In Indian Vaastu first of centre-point (Brahmasthan) is determined and this aspect has been discussed in considerable details in Indian Vaastu, while nothing of sort exists in Feng Shui.

20) East and north-east directions are considered as the most appropriate places for water preservation, reservoirs, well because Sun rays first of all in these directions. Continuous flow of Sun rays cleans and detoxifies pollutant and impure water. Sunrays also do not let bacteria and worms hatch in water. If there is darkness, due to absence of Sun rays, water gets toxic and polluted.

This way we find that the Indian Vaastu Science is perfectly sceintific and every aspect of it is replete and enriched by theory of cause and effect. So, we should feel indebted to our ancient ascetics for the amount of hard labour, research, invention and their divine knowledge. The Chinese Feng Shui considers south-east direction as the most appropriate place for water which concept has no scientifc basis and support.

(XXX) Pyramids

Q. What is implied by the term 'Pyramid'?

Ans. The term 'Pyramid' literally means — A Conical pillar or pole of 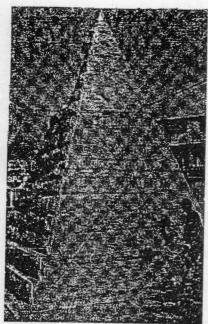 Stone. Some scholars breakup this word into parts, viz 'Pyra' and 'Mid' which means a triangular object through which fire or energy generates. In other words 'Pyramid' is a source of energy.

Q. Out of the five elements, which type of elements are attributed to the Pyramids?

Ans. Pyramid falls under sky or space element, that is 'Space energy'. This concept is employed to enhance space energy and light in a house.

Q. Are Pyramids solid structures?

Ans. No, Pyramid is never solid, because a solid Pyramid is a sort of burden on the earth and if it is so it can not have any magical and scintillating facilities and qualities. If there could be wonders in solid structures, then all the solid mountains could also possess scintillating qualities, but the fact is totally otherwise. Real fact remains that actual connection between space element and the energy flowing therein is the core factor. The Pyramids which are built in accordance with astrological and Vaastu principles are capable of possessing magical and wonderous power.

Q. How a person feels when he enters into a Pyramid?

Ans. A person, when he enters into a Pyramid, feels a sense of tranquility.

Q. From Where does energy generate in a Pyramid?

Ans. Pyramidal energy is situated in the centre point and its four corners and it moves upwards, from where it advances towards Pyramid point, whereas Sun-energy descends from the upward cone (top). Hence, a Pyramid gets its energy from both the centres—that is, solar energy comes down from top to bottom, and energy from the centre-point proceeds upwards.

Q. Where can solid energy be found in a Pyramid?

Ans. Solid Pyramid energy is found in the upper part of the pyramid and remains unaffected by other therapies and practices like Allopathy, Ayurveda, Accupressure, Yoga, Meditation or for that matter by any other therapy. See the following diagram.

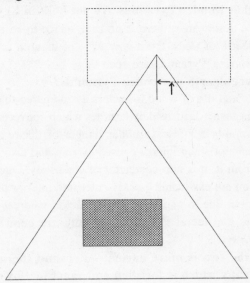

Q. Is it possible to derive monetary gains from Pyramids?

Ans. If a sanctified 'Lakhsmi Yantra' is kept under a pyramid and then kept in a cash-box or treasure chest, it will enhance income in a marvellous way. If this Yantra is 'Koormaprishtiya', it will show cent-percent benefic effects.

Q. What is the distinction between real Pyramids and Pyramid Yantras?

Ans. Real Pyramids resemble like residential houses. They are built with heavy and big stones and are used to protect the dead bodies. But small Pyramids are man-made and are processed with the help and power of Indian Science of Mantra and Tantra (emulets). These are imparted life with sanctified mantras, hence they possess magical and wonderful powers, even if they are small sized. Such small sized Pyramids are generally processed by using metal.

Q. Can Pyramids of Paper and Plastic can also be sanctified and imparted life?

Ans. No. Pyramids of paper and plastic can not be imparted consciousness by means of Mantra-power.

Q. Can wooden Pyramids also be used?

Ans. Certainly. But wood of only sacred trees should be utilised in processing wooden Pyramids. Any type of wood, whose use is prohibited by the treatises, should never be used.

Q. How is it that wooden Pyramids are not built in Egypt?

Ans. Egypt is a desert area, there is no rain, hance there are no trees, or there is absolute dearth of trees. Even now 97% of its area is manifested by desert, hence no wooden Pyramids are seen there.

Q. Why is there dearth of wooden Pyramids?

Ans. Durability and life of wood is far less as compared to metal, because wood decay and it is easily destroyed by termites which converts it into powder form. Wooden Pyramids are always under danger of decay and distortion. Morecover, wood cannot stand impact caused by rain and also scorching heat of the sun. Apart from it, it is non-conductor of electricity. Due to this reason solar energy rays can not easily and quickly enter into interior portion of wood through its top portion due to bad conductivity factor, whereas this is not the possibility in stone and metal Pyramids, as both are good conductors of electricity and sun-rays.

Q. Which of the two is more ancient—Pyramid therapy or Indian 'Shri-Yantra' therapy which is fortified and sanctified by tantra?

Ans. The Egyptians themselves maintain that their Pyramids are not older, as those were built around 2600 years B.C ., hence it is certain their Pyramids are not older than the given duration, whereas Indian Science of Emulets is far ancient than the Egyptian Pyramids.

(XXXI) MISCELLANEOUS TOPICS

Here I will throw light on those topics and problems which have not been dealt with in the preceding chapters.

Q. Why should not sit under a beam?

Ans. Here I will refer to a mythological legend of Hiranyakashyap and Prahlad. According to the legend, Hiranyakashyap was killed in the evening (called 'Sandhyaakaal' when the Sun is about to set and the moon is about to appear). So, taking a lesson and clue from the above mentioned legend, which appeared about 2000 years B.C., it was concluded that nobody should sit under a beam, girdar, and construction work of a building is not undertaken in the evening time. Sitting under a beam is like inviting death, misfortune, inauspicion and also shortening of life span.

To build an office under a beam, keeping a revolving chair or a seat is not considered good, as it creates adverse situations and also scuttles and impedes progress in an ongoing work and activity. Since beam itself remains under stress, it does not let a person work smoothly and keep him tension ridden also. If there is no other option than to sleep or sit under a beam, following corrective steps are advised to be adhered to,

1. Comouflge cealing of beam with tiles.

2. Vaastu-doshanashak Ganpati (of green colour) be attached on both sides of the beam.

3. If a flute each is hung on both sides of the beam, it will remove ominous effects caused by the beam.

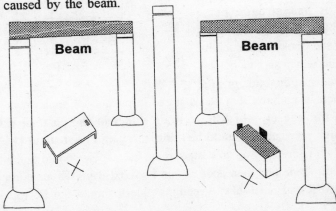

Q. Which is an ideal place for parking vehicles?

Ans. Parking place can be provided for in the south-east, away from the eastern wall and the house, and / or in the north-west direction, but away from the northern side of boundary wall and the house. If it is built in the south-west direction, then it should not touch the western and southern walls. If it is built in the south-west corner, then it should not touch the southern and western walls, but the plinth of internal surface be elevated higher. See the following diagram. These suggestions pertain to office & factory premises.

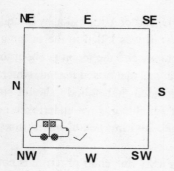

If parking is to be provided in a house, the most suitable direction will be north-west corner. If north-west corner is not available, then parking can be made in the south-east direction, but no parking place should exist in the north-east direction. Parking place can also be provided in the western and southern direction, but slope of parking surface should be towards north side.

Q. Is it not an ominous sign if a beehive exists in the house or the boundary wall?

Ans. Do not let a beehive exist in the house or in the boundary or in any other place in the house, as the bees can sting the children and others, due to their poisonous stings.

Q. It is maintained that water should not be kept in the south-west direction, why is it so?

Ans. It has already been mentioned that there should not be an 'Overhead Tank' in the south-east. Hence water should not be stored in the said direction or in a pit. But there is no harm if water is stored in pitchers or stonewares.

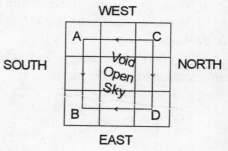

Q. In the houses, which have main doors in the eastern side, how and in which way rooms should be built, entry and exist should be made?

Ans. In a house, having an eastern main gate, room should be built in the north-east direction and then door should be fixed. But, if rooms are built in the north-west and north-east directions, doors should not be fixed in the south-east and north-east direction.

In the houses, having southern main gate, room should be built in the south-east direction, but do not affix any gate in the south-west direction.

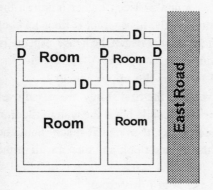
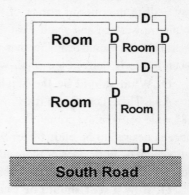

Note : In eastern main gate, entry should be from south-west. If room is built in the south-east and north-east directions, entry should be from south-east. In houses, which have main gate in the south, entry should be from southern side of south-east direction.

Q. Which should be the entry points in the rooms of such houses whose main doors lie in the north and west directions?

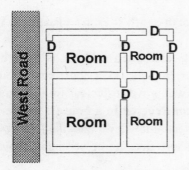
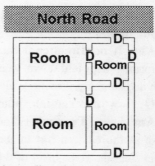

If a house has its main gate in the northern direction, rooms should be built in the south-west and north-west directions and entry should be from northern side of north-east direction.

In a house, which has its main gate in the western direction, rooms should be built in the south-east and south-west directions, and entry should be from western side of north-west direction.

Q. Which precautions are necessary in the house construction?

175

Ans. Precautions are imperatively essential. Leave enough vacant space all around the house and then start building construction. 1) When a sub-house has been built, it should not be divided into two parts 2) Do not raise any wall in the interior corner of the house and 3) Keep higher plinth in the southern, western and south-west directions of the house, that is floor level of the sub-house should be higher than the floor level of rest of the house, especially when house is built in the south-west direction.

Q. What should be the height of walls in the upper storey?

Ans. There is no harm if 18" wide walls of the first storey are raised over 18" wide walls of the ground floor. If it is not feasible but if the wall of the first floor is desired to be built 14" or 9" wide (thick), then equal space should be left vacant on both sides of the walls at the ground floor, and then a wall of the desired width can be built.

Q. How a seat should be built in the south direction?

Ans. You can raise / build a seat all along the southern direction, but its plinth level must be higher than the floor level of the house.

Q. How to construct a verandah in the north direction?

Ans. Level of verandah should be lower than the plinth level of the house.

Q. Can a house be built after filling up a water pond?

Ans. A house can be built in any direction (like south-east, south, south-west, west and north-west directions), after water-ponds have been duly filled in.

Q. It is said that east-west and north-south sites are also good. What is your opinion?

Ans. If no directional fault exists and when a house is built in the comformity with laid down Vaastu rules, in that case, a house can be built in north and southern directions also, as it will prove auspicious for the residents.

Q. How a verandah should be constructed in a house?

Ans. Floor of verandah should be kept at low level than the floor-level of house in the eastern but in the south-east flooring of verandah should be higher than the floor level of the house.

Q. What results will follow if a house (built up) is partitioned?

Ans. It has often been observed that, when there is more of brothers in the built up house, partition is affected. But, such a partition results in progress of one brother but loss of an another. See the following diagram.

In the diagram, in one portion, there is no space towards the south, whereas east and west directions are open. Due to this partition, the occupant of this partitioned portion will derive benefit. In the second case though the second

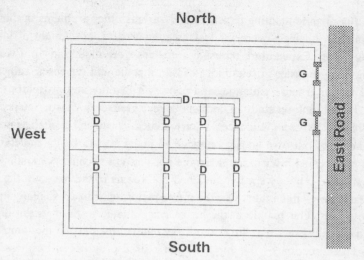

North

West

South

East Road

occupant has open and vacant space in the south, but the north side is blocked, hence it will constitute a Vaastu fault.

Hence such type of partitions are bad. As far as possible a built up house should not be partitioned and divided. So, it is better if a house is built on any already purchased plot of land.

Q. How does Vaastu Science casts its impact on personal life of a person?

Ans. In this context I refer to the woes expressed by Ms. Neena Gupta (of Kanpur), who is a housewife.

I have experienced many experiences in the context of Vaastu Science during my life. I inspected so many houses, without being noticed, with reference to truths and facts enshrined in Vaastu Science. I also experienced and felt certain experiences in the context of my own house which I relate hereunder.

"The day I was married, I experienced and found in my house nothing except illness. I rarely fell ill in my pre-marital life but, from the third day of my married life, I was afflicted with jaundice. All the members in my in-law's house were inflicted with one desease or the other. My husband had problem in the liver, my father-in-law and brother-in-law were operated upon. Then I also delivered a female child after an operation. After birth of my baby, she also fell ill, my father-in-law had to be operated upon once again. Though there was much progress in business, yet expenses exceeded the income. My newly wedded sister-in-law also had been remaining ill. When a son was born after some time, he too, started remaining ill. This way there was no respite

177

from illness and mounting expenses and various other problems in the family. Profits from business were far less as compared to the amount of labour of efforts put in. Expenditure on useless matters were mounting. In a way ther was nothing in order in relation to health, income and expenses, rather entir house was in a tense situation, and none was healthy and prosperous."

"Then I took up study in correspondence course in Vaastu Science, unde Dr. Bhojraj Dwivedi's guidance. When I studied Vaastu and applied its principle in the case of our own house, I noticed so many Vaastu faults and flaws. Ou house was rented prior to my marriage but was got vacant six months prior t my marriage. There were two attached bathrooms in the house at the time o my marriage — this I think was the prime factor that caused so many problem in the family. Our temple in the house was situated in the western directio So, first of all I rectified direction of the temple, by shifting the temple to tl north-east direction — this modification caused progress in business all of sudden and such a progress surfaced for the first time. The fire place (burne was situated alongside the western wall of the kitchen. I corrected the annual due to which diseases waned."

"After a year I also corrected Vaastu faults in my husband's shop. I set order temple and seat which resulted progress in business. Now all the membe in the family recognise the role played by removal of Vaastu faults. But ev now, a number of Vaastu flaws and faults still exist in our house. For instan the biggest fault lies in the north-east direction, as this direction is burdened the optimum. Garage, stairs, godown and lift are also in the north-east directic In order to dispel the said Vaastu faults I hung a "Vaastu Mangalkari Yantra" the shop (which was a part of the house) Installation of this Yantra yield auspicious signs in the first day itself, due to hopping sale on the first da followed by normal sales in the subsequent day, as per market conditions am quite hopeful that when north-eastern Vaastu faults are dispelled in t house, in near future, situations will improve."

Q. Is there any interrelation between Vaastu Science and a perso fate, as many persons are still leading a happy and prosperous life desp Vaastu faults? How is it?

Ans. Whenever a house is built some Vaastu faults do surface but so Vaastu rules are also followed, even if unknowingly. But there is an insepara interrelation between Vaastu and fate.

1. Favourable and good fate is the result of favourable and good Vaas
2. Unfavourable and bad fate is the result of unfavourable and bad Vaas

That is to say that if luck of a resident in a house is good, then the par which he lives, will yield benefic results and also that his life will be impacted favourably in that portion of the house where Vaastu principles have been adhered to, even of unknowingly. But as soon as the fate is unfavourable and planetary positions also change for the worse, the same person will start experiencing adverse effect of Vaastu faults.

Hence, if a person is happy and prosperous, despite unfavourable Vaastu faults, it is only uptil the time his good luck and stars favour him. He must have been far happier and prosperous had he been living in a house where Vaastu faults do not exist. In the later situation, when luck and Vaastu are favourable, he would have derived the benefits, in proportion to the efforts put in by him which were not possible had he been living in house which was afflicted with Vaastu faults.

If Vaastu of a house seems to be in order and without any faults, there are still chances that some of the Vaastu faults might have existed. If such persons are suffering, they are suffering due to their adverse planetary positions. If such persons live in a house, where Vaastu faults exist, they would have faced far more serious problems.

Hence, we can easily conclude if a house is built in accordance with Vaastu principles, then a person's fate can also change for the better **Effect of Vaastu Science.**

Q. Is Vaastu Science meant exclusively for the Hindus only, but not for the Muslims & Christians?

Ans. Vaastu is a science. As gravitational power of the earth cast equal effect on all persons, without any discrimination of caste, creed, colour or race, so do the magnetic rays equally cast their impact on all the human beings, irrespective of religion, caste, creed, colour or place. Moreover if any person or species of animals and birds are unaware of Vaastu and its principles, effect will be alike in all the living beings, including plants, trees and other vegetations. So, in this same manner, Vaastu science also casts its impact on all the living beings and it hardly matters whether it is an animal, boy or girl, or whether he has any faith or belief in this science. Each person is affected by good or bad results of Vaastu. Hence, we can conclude that Vaastu impacts Hindus, Muslims, Christians and all else equally, without any discrimination whatsoever.

Q. Which type of trees should not be planted in the premises of a house and factory?

Ans. This question has already been referred to earlier and suitably replied, hence please refer to preceding pages in the relevant context.

Dr. Bhojraj Dwivedi
A multi-dimensional Personality

He was born on September 5, 1949 in Dundhara, a village in Udaipur district of Rajasthan. He passed M.A. (Sanskrit) examination in 1st division and is a Ph.D in Astrology and also holds a D.Litt. degree. He was married to Smt. Janki Devi on March 5, 1977 and is proud father of two daughters and one son.

Dr. Dwivedi has written about 140 books. He also publishes 'Agyata Darshan' which is a fortnightly publication and 'Shri Chand Martand' Panchang, is published and edited by him for the last 24 years. He writes in Hindi and most of his books have been translated in English. Some of his famous books are "Thumb-The Mirror of your Fate", "Mystical World of Gems", "Kaalsarpayoga", "Remedial Vaastu", "Jyotish and Dhanyoga", "Study of omens", "Sampurna Vaastu Shastra" etc.

He has attended many conferences in India and foreign countries, attended T.V. interviewes, published many articles in renowned journals. He founded "All India Joytish Patrakar Parishad" (Regd.), "International Vaastu Association". He has also established" "Agyata Darshan Super Computer Services" through astrological problems of clients are addressed to and solved. He made predictions to the extent of 2768, in connection with national and international events and personalities and were published by popular news papers, magazines etc, and most of his predictions proved correct — this is such a remarkable landmark that has not, so far, been surpassed, or ever equalled, by any one else.

He undertakes "Vaastu Visits", in order to suggest remedies, for removal of vaatu defects, in houses, buildings, factories, industries and business enterprises. The readers can also acquire, both theoretical and practical knowledge, from the 12 books, written on various facets of Vaastu Science by the author.

Dr. Dwivedi also deals in the sale of gems, stones and 'Rashi-Ratna' fortune enhancing rings and lockets which are sanctified by suitable mantras. In addition, he is an expert in performing 'Karma-Kand', worship, recitation etc. The readers may avail of the opportunity, as per prescribed norms and fee, by a prior appointment, if they so desire.

Reserch work on various subjects, such as astrology, palmistry, Vaastu Feng Shui, Pyramids, ancient religions treastises, Ayurveda etc. is an ongoing process and various scholars are lending a helping hand in this respect.

Dr. Dwivedi is a multi-dimensional personality who has acquired great name and fame in India and abroad. His books are read with great interest and the Press and Public are highly appreciative of his multifaceted knowledge and expertise.

— *Publisher*

Gratitude

My first book, entitled 'Jyotish Mein Bhavan, Vaahan Ka Kirtiyoga' was first published in 1992. Then it was followed by "Sampurana Vaastu Shastra". "Commercial Vaastu", "Remedial Vaastu", and "Paryavaran Vaastu" and the readers approbated all my books. These books have been translated in English by Pt. Shiv Sharma who has rendered a yeoman's service in doing full justice to the related subjects. Other books on Astrology, Palmistry and Feng Shui have also been translated by him. So, my grateful gratitude to him.

Shri Narendra Kumar Ji, Managing Director of **Diamond Pocket Books,** has been constantly encouraging and motivating me to write books on various subjects which have, not so far, been dealt with suitably. So, I will always remain indebted and obliged to him for his motivation, assistance and guidance. But for him, so many books might not have seen even light of the day.

I had to take help and depend upon the information provided in the following books and I express my heartfelt gratitude to all the authors, publishers, magazines, journals, news papers etc. who have stood me in good stead.

This book is the very first book of its kind on the subject and I have tried my best to provide maximum authentic information on many important facts of Vaastu Shastra (Science) and also I have drawn comparison with Feng Shui and Pyramid philosophy. I have discussed, in fairly good details about the Vaastu problems of readers and whatever I have written is based on my personal experience and acquired knowledge. Hopefully this book will serve the intended purpose and serve as a guide to the readers who have already built their houses or plan to build their houses. Most of the Vaastu faults and flaws can be easily rectified by minor changes, without resorting to any wear and tear of the built up house / building.

Reference Books

1. 'Feng Shui Essence'—By Vijay Lakshmi Muiocho, Srishti Publishers and Distributers, New Delhi.
2. 'Vaastu Prashanottari'—by Gauri Tirupathi Reddy, Bangalore.
3. 'Interior Design with Feng Shui'—by Ryder, Published by An Imprint of Randum Century Group Ltd. London.

In addition to the authors of above referred books I am also equally grateful to those persons who had assisted me during my various journeys, in India and abroad, though it is not physically possible to mention their names individually, hence my unqualified apologies.